£5
SIGNED
—14

Sandra!

We did it! Now we're authors....

love'n'stuff
from
[illegible]

AMATEUR OF LiFE AND DEATH

Douglas John Thorp

W10

WARD 10
BOOKS

First edition – November 2015

Published in the United Kingdom by
Ward 10 Books
18A Orleans Road
London SE19 3TA

A CIP catalogue for this book is available from the British Library

ISBN 978-0-9934343-0-3

Designed and typeset by Ursula McLaughlin
ursula.mcl@gmail.com

Printed and bound by TT Litho Printers Ltd, Rochester, Kent

theidleeye.wordpress.com

Writers often use this spot to dedicate their work to their nearest and dearest, to those who have supported them from the outset and, on occasion, randoms who were there by default. As I can't think of anyone appropriate enough to be endorsed here, I'd like to pledge this waste of trees to the Edinburgh Donkey Sanctuary (if indeed it exists), as my father once told me that's where my inheritance would be going if there was anything left.

Acknowledgements

Without the support and (more importantly) hard cash from the following lovely people, this book would have remained in the darker recesses of my head, along with all the other half-baked ideas that will never see the light of day:

Alison Czajkowskyj, Maureen Moore, Melinda Doring, David McClelland, Fiona Perry, Mark Dicey, Gary Clements, Zee Zomorrodian, Lara Newton-Clare, Gill Bailey, Paul Cope, Rita Radovanovitch, Ludovic Merle, Helen Raison, Donald Ross Skinner, Juliet Mayo, Peter Woollard, Simon Phipps, Mark Perry, Nick Johnson, Will Foster, Nick Woollard, Peter Walker, Mark Bynon, Jane Bynon, Trish Dicey, Nick Whillis, Sheila Deasey, Lisa Carpenter, Stephen Thorp, Ambrose Chapel, Sioux Fern Durow, Philippa Burne, Nics Reeve, Neil Howman, Jonathon Hall, Aziza Azul Walker, Claudia Fiocchetti, Jo Mulvagh, Patrick Mangan, Margaretta Jolly, Bianca Madden, Tom Harle, Valerie Astles, Laura Hinde, Kate Thorp, Laura Marchant-Short, Olivia Pos, Denise Connelly, Sally Mason, Rachel Burchell, Nancy Dicey, John Dicey, Julitha Ryan, Xav Rees, Charlie Hutchinson, John Bynon, Elinor Perry-Smith, Kirstin Stromberg, Sarah Johnson, Emma Jardine, Cyrus Gilbert-Rolfe, Nicola Cutcliffe, Claire Thorn, Mark Hutchinson, Jenny Granville, Katherine Henderson, Darren Wilkin, Ben Aitken, Ken Rutherford, Lucy Quinnell, Pål Nisja-Wilhelmsen, Simon Bailey, Jessie Doring, Nigel Dean, Grant Butcher, Matthew Bailey, Voy Leedale, Maggie McLaughlin, Aki Yamada, David Parsons, Caroline Crome, Gillian Beail, Charles Swallow, Martin Ampoman, Nina and Andrea @ Comfort and Joy, Esme @ Bodhagaia.

Additional thanks to:

Kickstarter (for the platform)

Dan Laidler (for cover artwork and defining me in one image)

Donald Ross Skinner and Rupert Ingham (for all things audio)

Sarah Johnson (for helping me get it out there)

James Norton (for your much better introduction)

Gavin Skinner (for the shameless steal)

Elinor Perry-Smith (for proofreading and calming me down)

Karen and Laura @ Crystal Palace Food Market (for being aces)

Numidie Bar (for bearing with me when I did my first reading)

My brother Stephen (for letting me get away with it for so long)

Mo Bounechada (for author headshot)

Lucy Fogarty at TT Litho (for all things print)

New Zealand Marlborough Pinot Noir (for giving me hope where once there was none)

Ursula McLaughlin (for the time, effort and skill it took to make this book look the way it does)

Christopher Douglas, Andrew Nickolds, Jonathan Ames, Olivia Laing, David Thorne, Stewart Lee, John Fowles and David Sedaris amongst many others (for inspiration)

Finally, to all the artists (for contributing your astounding work)

Contents

Introduction

Me: *What's the difference between an introduction and a foreword?*

Friend: *Traditionally, somebody else writes the foreword and the author writes the introduction.*

Me: *Somebody else? Where's the point in that?*

Friend: *Well, they can put a different spin on it. You know, make it sound more important than it actually is.*

Me: *It is important!*

Friend: *You write it then.*

Me: *But you're saying that if I do, it won't carry as much weight. Look, this is my first book. I can't afford to screw it up.*

Friend: *Don't you know someone who likes your style and would be prepared to pitch in? It doesn't have to be too fancy, just get them to big you up a bit.*

Me: *My mum likes some of it. But she also thinks it's crass and unfunny in places. Not quite the message I'm trying to get across.*

Friend: *I guess not.*

Me: *Don't you know anyone?*

Friend: *I know your mum.*

Me: *This isn't helping any.*

Friend: *There are agencies that could do it for you. If there's only a few hundred words, it shouldn't cost all that much.*

Me: *So I pay someone who has never met me or read anything I've written to say how much they like what I do?*

Introduction

Friend: *Something like that, yes. Maybe you're too close to your own work to be properly objective.*

Me: *Hang on! I haven't spent the last eight months holed up in one room for someone else to come along and be objective about it. It is what it is and I'm not budging on that.*

Friend: *Don't have one then! It's not compulsory.*

Me: *It's a book. And books have introductions and forewords, they just do.*

Friend: *What's the matter with you? Loads of books don't have them. 'The Rolf Harris Picture Book of Cats', for starters.*

Me: *It's a picture book, that's why. And that preamble at the beginning is an excuse for him to cram in a load of cat photographs without having to write about them. So effectively it's an introduction, as well as being a construct.*

Friend: *Of course it's a construct! Most of these things are. What you're doing here is a construct.*

Me: *What do you mean?*

Friend: *The very fact that you're having a conversation with me – when everyone knows you've written it yourself – is a construct. And my guess is you'll use it as a lame substitute for the real thing.*

Me: *You disappoint me.*

Friend: *That's what friends are for.*

Me: *You don't get it, do you? There's a lot of hard facts I've got to include here and there isn't a lot of space. So why would I waste it on you?*

Friend: *On you go then. Promise me one thing though. I know you'll think it's terribly droll to write me in as a stooge, but it's been done to death. That whole 'exposing the framework' trick is desperately old hat. So if I were you, I'd avoid it. Like the plague.*

Me: *Thanks for the tip.*

Friend: *Don't mention it.*

***

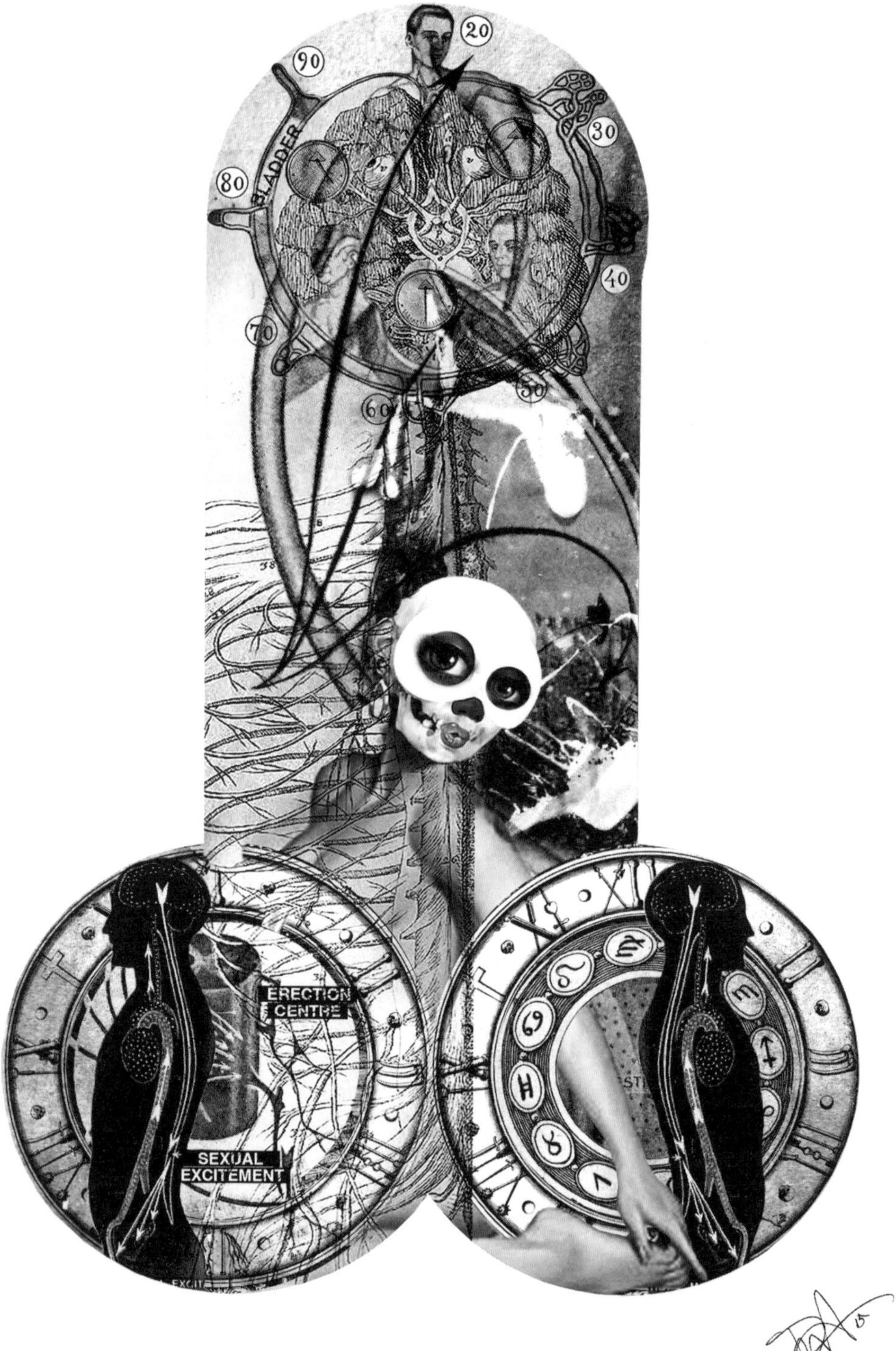
20
90
30
BLADDER
80
40
70
50
60
ERECTION
CENTRE
SEXUAL
EXCITEMENT

01

THE TYRANNY OF SEX

Not a lot needs to be said about this one, although there is a certain irony to me giving anyone at all advice in the bedroom department.

ILLUSTRATION:
THE DNA FACTORY

The Tyranny of Sex

One of the (very few) advantages of getting on a bit is that you are no longer governed by the incessant demands of your wretched, truculent body. Back in the day, you could be contentedly getting on with a hobby of your choice (let's say, for argument's sake, gardening) and the next thing you know, an inappropriate stamen is frantically transmitting lewd signals to the pathetic pink pudding between your ears, which in turn sends an emergency klaxon to the privates, instantly shutting off the master logic valve and leaving you rudderlessly navigating your way to an inevitably messy conclusion. You have no say in this. You are putty in the hands of a force deliberately cooked up by nature to humiliate you at all costs. This will pass, trust me.

You'll know you've come through the cloud layer when you begin to consider options:

'Yes, I could bust a blood vessel in a locked room upstairs in broad daylight at my eldest son's graduation party, or I could eat my own body weight in artisan cheese, neck a couple of bottles of Waitrose top-shelfers and pass out on the sofa as his mates search underneath me for a cab company flyer.'

This, although far from perfect, at least suggests that something is seeping through to the mainframe. But don't get out of your prams, there's still a long way to go.

To be fair, it does take a while for the pointless juices your reproductive system will insist on brewing, to simmer down enough for you to make an educated decision over what exactly to do about them. Overcompensation in the alcohol department is statistically a popular choice, as temporary stasis is infinitely preferable to the half-meant apologies one is forced to make the morning after whatever it was you did when you were slavering like a bull. *Saga Magazine* understands this implicitly, which is why they kindly start sending you a bewildering gadgets catalogue not long after your fiftieth birthday, championing electronic butter dishes and secure solutions to keep your soap dry. By the time you've worked out exactly what you're meant to do with the bloody things, any urges you may once have been slave to in your prime will be long gone. It is a stroke of marketing genius.

Based on the above, my advice to the young people is this: by all means, persevere with that sexting/Tinder/antisocial networking thing you all seem to like. It's harmless fun and your body won't know the difference between this and the real thing. And the salient point is that it serves as a useful segue between the tyranny of sex and liberation thereof you have yet to experience. Cyberfilth is the only working prophylactic you will ever need, protecting you from your revolting selves 24/7. Embrace it. The alternatives are far, far worse.

FORSALE

02

THE LUNAR TWITS
(HAVE TAKEN OVER THE ASYLUM)

Our insane property bubble taken to its intergalactic conclusion.

ILLUSTRATION:
URSULA MCLAUGHLIN

The Lunar Twits (Have Taken Over the Asylum)

Property prices getting a bit steep for you in that there London? Need to stick your flag into a chunk of affordable real estate almost certain to appreciate wildly over the course of several lifetimes? Well guess what? You're in luck. The Lunar Registry is currently flogging off tracts of land on the Moon, complete with certificate of ownership, full mineral rights and a framed satellite photograph of your very own galactic Shangri-La for the unrepeatable knockdown price of $18.95 an acre.

'What could be greater than to own your own crater?'

Indeed.

Tempting though this offer may be, it might also be prudent to point out that many of us will be drawn to the more desirable hotspots of our celestial neighbour. For example, the Sea of Vapours is looking pretty tidy – *own front door, excellent transport links, ideal for first time buyer, no onward chain*. And unorthodox though it may seem at present, *Mare Vaporum* is likely to be a strong pull for artistic individuals priced out of the likes of Penge and Peckham Rye. Speculative buyers can therefore realistically expect a robust return on any investment made in advance of the inevitable gentrification process. In short, there's going to be a bunfight.

Let's presume I want to snap up a couple of acres in the Lake of Dreams, one of the most sought-after locations for adventurous romantics. *Lacus Somniorum* has, at best, ill-defined borders and includes the flooded impact craters *Mason* and *Plana* to the north. Which basically means I'll be pitching for the south-facing plots like everyone else. To say nothing of future boundary disputes, riff-raff moving into the neighbourhood and the division of maintenance duties once the conversions start:

'Turns out, them next door have discovered a rich seam of anorthite that runs directly through my back yard and I've only just had the bloody thing moonscaped. I'll be screwed if I'm going to help those nouveau-riche shysters any more than I have already, particularly after they only painted their half of the pod doorway. In orange, for Christ's sake! So petty! And while we're at it, the sinkhole's opened up again and guess who's mucking out the sulphur deposits? Now, I'm no pedant but it's basic human decency to keep the communal zones clear. Who else do they think does it? And as for the stink that comes out of their kitchen most nights, well really!'

In all honesty, *Lacus Somniorum* is probably not for me. And that goes for pretty much every must-have bolthole on the sodding thing. It will become the East Grinstead of the Solar System before you know it and I haven't got all that long left. So what to do? I'm thinking Pluto's looking like a good bet right now, as is the Heliopause and Eris if you can be arsed. Or simply wait for Foxtons to open their first gravity-free bar.

03

THE iNFERNAL LOOP OF LEEDS

I got caught in the monstrous Loop on the way to my father's memorial service. Despite getting to Leeds with time to spare, I never made it. And yes, I took it out on my car.

ILLUSTRATION:
ANTHONY REYNOLDS

The Infernal Loop of Leeds

When faced with events too harrowing to compute, the human brain slows everything around it down to a manageable speed, whilst enormous quantities of adrenalin are simultaneously secreted around the body in order to cope with any potential trauma. It is an extraordinarily sophisticated defence mechanism, initiated unconsciously and, for the most part, it works. But not always. Yesterday, I went to Leeds.

I'll begin with a caveat. If you've ever had faith in the notion that the fragile infrastructure of British urban planning will always be driven by some of the greatest minds in the field, think again – it's not. Anyone who has had the poor fortune to attempt navigating the West Riding's principal settlement by car will back me up on this. Leeds city centre is a vast, sprawling metropolis that has unsuccessfully stitched the very old to the very new, and neither one of them is gonna budge when it comes to compromise. How very Yorkshire! So when councillors Cox and Evans got involved with the CAD kids to keep the traffic flowing, the result was, and still is, one of the most dehumanising travesties of our time.

On arrival, it looks pretty slick. All the major arteries head neatly towards the centre, but before you know it you are force-fed into the obscenity that is the Loop. Here, the satanic offspring of Hieronymus Bosch and J.G. Ballard has been made flesh in the most destructive pact since the Coalition. Previous motorists, who have failed to correctly negotiate the Albert Speer-inspired horrorshow they have unwittingly stumbled upon, lie in various states of decomposition inside the cabs of their own vehicles; some taken violently by bitter, frustrated passengers and others by their own hand, the alternative being more of the same. And why is this? Well, put simply, because it is *IMPOSSIBLE* to get to wherever it is you need to be:

> ***Me:*** *I'd like to go over there, please.*
>
> ***Loop:*** *By all means. Now, veer off in the opposite direction until you come to a roundabout the size of Switzerland. You have approximately 0.6 seconds to decide which one of eight possible exits to take. All the signs will be at least 150 metres above the road and the traffic will be baying for your blood, so probably best to wing it. Oh dear, you've taken the by-road to Wakefield. Unfortunately you now have to drive 1.6 miles to the next exit and come back the opposite way. No, not down there, that's for buses and HGVs and will take you into the pedestrianised zone. Reverse down this one way street until you come to the next feed. Yes, it is busy so be careful. I'm afraid you'll have to head towards Ilkley until you come to another roundabout. I know, there's loads of them. When you've worked out which one I'm referring to, get into the left lane. Oh, you're in the right lane and there's four others to cross. Never mind, just do what everyone else does; pull up onto the verge, kick the crap out of your car, kick the crap out of anyone in the vicinity and weep like a baby. No amount of adrenalin can save you now…*

And yes, it's true – the whole shebang happens in torturous slow motion. It's her absolute, magnificent slap in the face. In Leeds, no one can hear you scream.

04

THE ANT

*This is what happens when you spend too much time alone.
Also why there are other people on the planet.*

ILLUSTRATION:
CLAIRE FLETCHER

The Ant

People say that your world shrinks or expands in direct parallel with your immediate environment. If you so happen to be the foreign policy minister of a suitably distressed nation, your brushstrokes will, by necessity, be rather broad. If, however, you are housebound for whatever reason, the tiniest of details can get magnified beyond all recognition, often becoming the primary focus of your day. And ever since I decided to seismically alter my own life parameters by switching an active job for one that ties me to the computer, my home kitchen has become an exotic new landscape, populated by minuscule, indigenous creatures with whom I must learn to cohabit. My favourite being the common ant, three of which I have become quite fond.

It starts at lunchtime. The minute that multipack of American-style bagels is in town, Dominic and Sophie (yes, they have names) get active, darting up to and away from the chopping board without so much as a by-your-leave. They do get on my tits a bit, so I have developed an early warning system, whereby I knock several times on the work surface and usually they get the message. Obama, on the other hand, does not. His remit is to push the envelope, which invariably he does by hopping up to the cucumber slices and flicking me a V sign. Fair enough, but I most certainly would not care for him to end his days in my sandwich. So I have words. Stern ones.

A grown man reprimanding a single ant for insubordination must appear somewhat irregular to the uninitiated. But rules are rules, no matter how diverse the cultural boundaries, and Obama would do well to take them on board. Being a big softie, I tend to let him off on the proviso he doesn't nose-dive into the coleslaw. Because then I'd get plain ugly. As well he knows.

Yesterday though, he pushed me too far. I had torn off the Marigolds and set them down by the sink. It's my way of saying *'In a few seconds I'm coming through with a J-Cloth. Steer clear.'* Dom and Soph totally got it as per, but Obama took umbrage and stood his ground. How exactly do you alert an over-cocky formicid to the real and present danger? That with one conclusive left swipe, I could create more havoc for the little shit than Hurricane Katrina or that big tsunami a while back, without batting an eyelid? Even the clattering of expensive Japanese knives and the sonic deterrent that is Milton Jones on Radio 4 did nothing to stem his tenacity. So I flipped. Crouching down so that our eyes were level, I blew him straight into the washing up bowl. And then apologised profusely.

There's been no sign of him today. He's definitely not dead, because I rescued him with a spatula and dried him down with kitchen paper. Probably sulking with Dom and Soph, I'd imagine. But we'll work something out.

2 LITTLE
LIVID BIRDS

05

THE ANGRY BIRDS

My love/hate relationship with Twitter perseveres unabated.

ILLUSTRATION:
MAGDA ARCHER

The Angry Birds

It's hard not to get incensed by all the stupid things people do. Whether they've voted wrong or looked at you funny, gone shopping with a ridiculous hipster hairdo or put their feet on the seats, it's enough to have you frothing at the gills most days. To be honest, it's exhausting. A quick spleen-vent at work or down the pub doesn't help much either, because there you'll find even more ephemera to get livid about. It's an infinite cycle of bile. A human centipede of perpetual fury. And once you're in it, there's no getting out. Without lithium. Or chocolate.

So where can like-minded hotheads meet and bleat when the going gets excruciating? Which crucible is robust enough to contain the white heat of contemporary rage? Yes, you guessed it, it's our old chum the Twitter. That stalwart portal, which gives with one hand and destroys with the other, is the paradoxical Shiva of the internet. But here it is not enough to simply rock up and pitch in, oh no! To be considered a player, you must have followers. Like Jesus. Or Charles Manson. When you finally get a few, you'll be needing a few more. And then more still. Until eventually, the very notion that these followers are actual people, as opposed to numerical online manifestations of your rampant unfettered ego, evanesces like a springtime morning mist.

Anyway, I was checking my feed this morning at 5.17am (I was up early, sick with worry that I'd forgotten to charge my phone), and noticed that I had been unfollowed. Only by one, but I felt the ricochet and was smarting from it. Having that extra bit of time on my hands, I spent the next few hours trawling through recent hard drive back-ups in order to expose and humiliate my perpetrator. '*Unfollow me?*' I thought. '*I'll learn ya!*' But this one was good.

Very good. Using what they call a cloaking address, xoigirl.vikki264 had manipulated my good nature into accepting her into the fold and giving her that most rare of opportunities to shine. Which, for reasons best known to herself, she had chosen to spurn.

Now don't get me wrong, I can handle rejection. It has been the very fabric of my existence since I told Helena Bonham-Carter's sister I had all my own teeth and hair in an introductory email. However, I'm super-sagacious these days. I had deliberately chosen to ignore her rather pneumatic avatar in favour of what I considered a more mature approach to online platonic relationships. That somehow, in the vein of *Pretty Woman*, she could have been persuaded to take the straight and narrow path. But it was not to be. To say nothing of the potential misinterpretation of my intentions. So now I find myself with a mere 33 followers and yes, I'm bloody spewing! Although ViaFlowers11 is looking promising, despite the cost of the visa.

06

THE MESSIAH

True story. However, the lady concerned 'went wee' all by and onto herself but it didn't suit the post. So I changed it. Like Jesus would have.

ILLUSTRATION:
NICK HOLLYWOOD

The Messiah

As some of you may know, I've been working in a Catholic church now for quite some time. My brief is to conserve the merchandise, the latest being a huge gilded reredos with exquisitely carved priests gazing up at a floating Lady of Suffering with her attendant cherubs and, a bit further up, God. With a massive beard. And a book.

Every day I arrive an hour or so before the morning Mass. To get to the scaffold, I have to push my bike past an elderly man lying prostrate on the floor in a state of reverie, touching the feet of a plaster cast of Our Lady with six plastic swords piercing her sacred heart. He barely notices me. Next, I nod graciously at the Silver Vixen (who smiles provocatively back) and then head on up to the tower. Usually I bail out for the Mass itself, but sometimes I catch the last of it. A priest in white and purple robes, looking and sounding like Mark E. Smith, finishes the proceedings by chanting the beginning of a hymn and then walking off to the sacristy in solemnity, leaving the congregation to wrap up the singing and depart. Which, for the most part, they do.

A few weeks ago, however, a straggler got locked in. She'd passed out on one of the pews and fell under the penetrating in-house security radar. When she came to, frightened and coming down off something, her first vision was that of myself, alone, at height and magnificently backlit by powerful halogens. The following exchange went something like this:

Me: *Are you all right?*

Lady: *Who… who are you? Do you want me to sing for you?*

Me: *Maybe not now. Do you know how to get out?*

Lady: *Are you Jesus?*

Me: *Er…*

Lady: *Let me sing for you, Jesus.*

Me: *I think we'd better...*

Lady: LET ME SING FOR YOU, JESUS!

Me: *OK. What can you do?*

Lady: *Tell me what to sing.*

Me: *Look, I'm really not Jesu...*

Lady: WHAT DO YOU WANT ME TO SING?

Me: *Um... How about Twinkle Twinkle Little Star? Do you know that one?*

Lady: *Just like you, Jesus. A twinkling star. In Heaven.*

Me: *Thank you. But I think you should speak to Father Pat first.*

Lady: *I wrote you a letter. Did you get my letter?*

Me: *I don't think so.*

Lady: *I gave it to Our Lady. She kept it for you.* SHE KEPT IT FOR YOU!

Me: *I'll ask her for it later.*

Lady: *I need to go wee.*

Me: *Wait a minute. I'll come down and show you...*

Lady: HELP ME GO WEE, JESUS! HELP ME GO WEE!

So I did. I helped the lady go wee. And then we took a short walk together to the Chelsea and Westminster Hospital where she was taken in and my services superseded by those more qualified than I. Because I'm not Jesus, I'm just a fella.

P155 OFF

07

THE CARB UNCLE

Did every male in the country drive a bloody Triumph in the '60s? They made shedloads of the things and yet I seem to have encountered every last bastard one of them.

ILLUSTRATION:
DAN LAIDLER

The Carb Uncle

One of the downsides to owning a classic car is that people will insist on talking to you about it. Whether you're underneath it, inside it or getting out, invariably you will be approached by an enthusiastic cardie type with battered NHS glasses, aching for a lengthy exchange about horsepower, turning circles and the good old days when they '*made things proper*'.

It goes with the territory. And for reasons completely beyond me, there is an unspoken presumption that you care as deeply about engines and distributors and carburettors *and all the other stuff that gets greasy every time you look at it and ruins your good trousers because you thought you'd only have a quick tinker but it's never quite that simple is it*, as they do.

You can see them approaching a mile off, all dewy-eyed, drooling and preparing for their inevitable opening gambit:

> **Carb Uncle:** *Used to have one of them meself, mate. First car, she was. Went like a rocket. And you could turn her on a sixpence. Lovely motor. Had her long?*
>
> **Me:** *About ten years.*
>
> **Carb Uncle:** *We got ours in… er… when did we get ours, Joyce?*
>
> **Joyce:** *1967. Our honeymoon.*
>
> **Carb Uncle:** *That's right! '67 it was. Took her down the Costa del Sol, never had no trouble. Well, I say no trouble but you know what it's like. Like to play up sometimes, don't they? But the beauty of the old 'uns is you can do the work yourself, right? Flip up the bonnet, sit on the wheel and get stuck in. Not like your modern rubbish. First sign of trouble and it's all 'computer says no! No way José!' Tell you what, mate, I'd give ten of any car on the road right now for one of those. 'Cos they made them proper back then. Right, Joyce?*

Joyce: *Yes, dear.*

Carb Uncle: *Lovely engines 'n' all. Yours a two litre?*

Me: *Yes.*

Carb Uncle: *Twin carbs?*

Me: *Yes.*

Carb Uncle: *Strombergs?*

Me: *Yes.*

Carb Uncle: *Your Stromberg was the king of carbs, make no mistake. Tune 'em to within an inch of their life, I should coco. Mind you, they couldn't half give you strife on the long haul. Spent many an hour on the hard shoulder with a spanner or two in the jacksie pocket, ain't that the truth, Joyce?*

Joyce: *Yes, dear.*

Back then, I learned to actively engage with these people. How I would laugh at the absurdities of modern vehicles. How I pretended to yearn for the golden era of motoring, when one could take to the open road in a car proudly manufactured in Great Britain, safe in the knowledge that it was the envy of the developed world. But these days, I'm afraid I couldn't give a toss. Because if I give Carb Uncle the kind of time he's after, I'll never get the bloody thing sorted. And I'm off to France next week. So please, could you just piss off?

08

THE WINDOWS TO THE SOUL

Dad, if you're reading this up there, thanks. I owe you.

ILLUSTRATION:
MATT JEFFS

The Windows to the Soul

When he put his mind to it, my father had a great smile. It was one of those magnificently craggy ones, as pioneered by W.H. Auden towards the end of his own years, which dug huge trenchlines into the soft tundra of his face and suggested, whether it was true or not, that he was kind, and genuinely delighted to have you as company. Yorkshire Television was quick to pick up on this most saleable of assets, so in pretty much every publicity shot taken from the 1980s onwards, you can see him attempting to squash his nose hard into the well of his cheekbones, like some sort of demented human Corby trouser press, whilst simultaneously keeping his eyes open and looking sexy. And, unlikely though this may sound, for the most part he pulled it off.

As the firstborn of four, I have inherited (to a lesser extent) something similar. When the appalling fissures first appeared I was horrified, so desperate was I to preserve the illusion of youth. Snaking their way across my cheeks like levees towards the ocean, they became impertinent reminders of my own mortality, which I bitterly resented. But as the years rolled on, I kind of grew into them, accepted them, and now I shall ruthlessly exploit them for my own financial gain. Hear me out.

I've only ever had publicity shots done once. It was back in the '90s, when I was trying to look moody and angst-ridden for an art-rock band that I fronted. The fact that we never got picked up, and that the photographs fell into the dustbin of insignificance, was clearly down to the fact that I was not yet ready to face the full-frontal glare of fame and fortune. And possibly because a previous night's drinking had made my eyes look like pissholes in the snow. But now I am older, wiser and sly as you like. So, what if I harness Dad's old ruse for the back cover of this book that I'm doing? That, instead of going all Charles Bukowski on you, I could make you believe I'm enormous fun to hang out with? Simply by wrinkling up my face! It works across the board – the oldies will think they can trust me, and the young people will find me endearing. Sexy, even.

Now, I've been practising in front of the bathroom mirror, but I think the silver must have buckled. When I scrunch up one side (leaving the other unwrinkled and all come-hither), it looks like I'm having a stroke. Yet if I go for both at once, the eyes are lost in a sea of unsightly crevices. And the eyes, as any fule kno, are the windows to the soul. I've even tried the direct approach, looking straight into camera with a slight hint of crumpled world-weariness. But I just come across as a massive tool. And we can't have that, can we?

09

THE BODY BEAUTIFUL

Although we cannot halt the ageing process, we should never be reminded of it in our more vulnerable moments. I'm sorry, but 1970s – what were you thinking?

ILLUSTRATION:
MARTIN RIDGWELL

The Body Beautiful

I have a distant memory of my mother's bathroom in the 1970s. I'm pretty sure it had turquoise carpet throughout (right up to the unit borders), and around the bath itself was a set of those mirrors which disappeared into infinity. I mention these because I've rarely seen anything similar since, and it did strike me at the time that they were curious things to have at all: the very notion that anyone would willingly install a primitive version of CCTV, seeking out and exposing every hideous flaw the human body can cook up, brutally illuminated under the unforgiving scrutiny of a 150W bulb encased inside an upside-down jelly mould, did seem rather odd. But, I was only about eight. At that age, you get things wrong.

I hadn't, though. This last bank holiday weekend saw me ensconced with fine friends inside an Edinburgh Airbnb. It had one bathroom and yes, in what probably was a nod to the retro accoutrements of yesteryear, it also had the very same fitted mirrors. Which meant I could see my own sorry bottom snaking into the distance more times than I would care to discuss. The horrors did not stop there. When was the last time you had a proper look at your own body in its entirety? Not recently, I'd wager. As I wrestled with the shower head, and made silent prayer that the glass would steam up smartly under the surge of its own revulsion, I noted that the ageing process had effectively morphed my once relatively well-proportioned frame into something out of *Lord of the Rings*.

The torso looked like an afterthought. Squat, pushing out in areas I previously didn't know existed and to these eyes, shamefully unaesthetic, it sat uncomfortably above two vulgar flesh potatoes, crushed mercilessly out of shape by the passage of time and the ongoing onslaught of Marlborough Pinot Noir. Not being load-bearing in their own right, the buttocks had clearly begged the legs below for reinforcement, but sadly to no avail; consequently, some chronic subsidence was evident at the join, probably worthy of one of those Heritage grants if I'd got my act together. Not to mention the hilarious thinning pin that balanced precariously on top of all the above. The entire gruesome shooting match was a David Attenborough documentary on the decline of Western human anatomy, realised in Kinder Egg Surprises. And directed by ISIS.

Now, I know we're all supposed to accept the deterioration of the body as standard. That the vanity of youth should disappear in a plume of dust if one has any dignity at all. But if you could have seen what I saw in those ridiculous mirrors, I do honestly believe you might think again. When confronted with the genuinely shocking, we tend to be genuinely shocked. As I was. Which is why, from now on, I shall be taking my showers in the dark.

ZZZ

10

THE WOLF OF WEST NORWOOD

Scorsese's Wolf of Wall Street was doing the rounds, rubbing salt into the open wounds of old gits like me. So I flung a bit back.

ILLUSTRATION:
RICHARD CRIGHTON

The Wolf of West Norwood

'See that two bedroom flat in a quiet residential area about eight miles from where it's at? That's mine (when I pay off the mortgage in 15 years). I also own a decaying car that's older than me, take painkillers once a day if the back's playing up and still owe £132 in council tax. When I was 26, I was selling sandwiches off a bicycle in the Farringdon area for less money than my niece makes in an afternoon, couldn't hold down a girlfriend and drank myself to sleep most nights. Like it?'

On reflection, perhaps I've left it too late to enjoy the nefarious lifestyle portrayed by Jordan Belfort in Martin Scorsese's latest epic. Sadly, the days of ludes, ladies and Lamborghinis are long gone, but the thirst for excess never completely abandons you, particularly if you haven't had it in the first place. So here's a checklist for any senior slickers out there that will not hand over the baton:

Wellman 50 Plus: *The holy grail of oral healthcare. Neck one of these beauties with a couple of Omega 3s and you'll come up smiling for 24 hrs. What's more, you can drive all you like and still operate the Stannah. Recommended.*

Acme Pool Cleaning: *If you do happen to get caught short at an all-important client meeting, these guys are discreet, fast as lightning and have on-site fabric care facilities. Includes Dralon®.*

Ladbrokes: *You like to gamble. But that itch never got properly scratched, right? Well guess what? Instead of pissing away your blue-collar quids on the never-never, these horses will keep on comin' atcha until the end of time. Simply smoke 5000 tabs a week, lie to your wife like you used to and blow the housekeeping fund in less time than it takes to say 'divorce'.*

Saga Magazine: *No more Hustler, no more Penthouse. But keep it real with Saga, the only monthly you can read under the duvet by torchlight without getting your head stoved in. Now subtly laminated for guilt-free enjoyment.*

Viking-Direct Office Supplies: *Sell me this pen.*

Fred Olsen: *What's this? Are you serious? A yacht! (With maids, cooks, 1300 paying guests, easy access toilets on all levels and occasional live music and/or comedy in the theme bar).*

Methuselah Homes UK: *When your hellraising days are finally behind you, why not reminisce with like-minded chums in one of our 'off the beaten track' tailor-made units? Don't worry, we'll change your name and contact details for you, it's all part of the service.*

And for all of the above, there is no fee. We wrinklies must stick together, rallying fervently against the relentless onslaught of youth and taking whatever tablets they give us to keep us going. Senility is a state of mind, not an ailment. You can have that one. You're welcome.

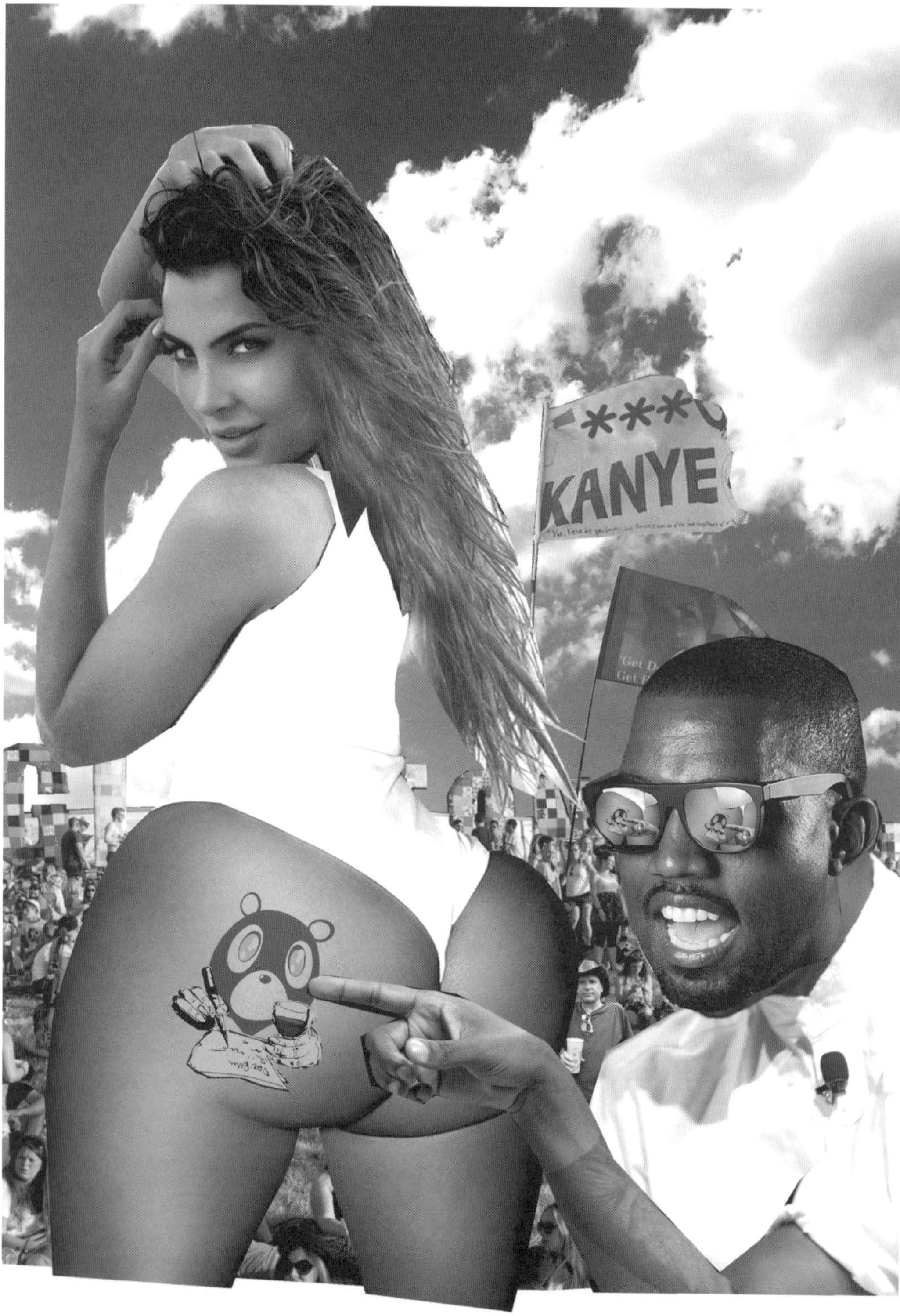
KANYE

11

THE KANYE CONSPIRACY

I'm proud to declare I still haven't heard a single song by this person. Or his big-bottomed wife. At Glastonbury, I ended up talking bollocks to Flame Proof Moth and drinking overpriced cider until he was done. For which, I'm told, he will sue.

ILLUSTRATION:
PETER QUINNELL

The Kanye Conspiracy

Remember last year? Me neither, which is the predominant reason I churn out this self-indulgent effluent every week. So that, in a quiet moment of the day when the wine fog has lifted, I can claw back clues as to my activities over the last three and a half years, and make out I have near-perfect recall. Yes, like that bloke out of *Neighbours* (what was his name?) in *Memento*. So, imagine my surprise when I discovered I had attended the Glastonbury festival. Quite willingly, apparently. Can that be right? And why on earth would I have agreed to such a thing, being as I am rather ancient and unsuitably constructed for the al fresco activities of youth?

I dug a little deeper, only to find out that, to my horror, I am going again in June. And that I have already shelled out perfectly good moolah for the privilege. What fresh hell is this? If ever there was a deterrent to the perils of Pinot… Anyway, my fate being sealed thus, I thought it prudent to at least find out exactly who I shall be forced to watch, and in narratively convenient fashion, the organisers announced yesterday that someone called Kanye West will be headlining on the big stage. Kanye West? Who the shoo is she? I thought it was a holiday destination for wealthy folk, somewhere near the Keys in Florida. And whilst I realise I no longer fit the festival demographic, you'd think they could at least meet me halfway – the Bay City Rollers still have a bit of spunk left, and young people can mock them on the Twitter if they get bored.

Seeing as I already had my detective hat on, I discreetly asked my niece to get me up to speed, ignorance being no excuse in these matters:

Poppy: *Are you for real?*

Me: *Yes, I think so.*

Poppy: *No, I mean you've never heard of Kanye West?*

Me: *I haven't. Does that make me a bad person?*

Poppy: *He's only the biggest rapper in the world!*

Me: *Rapper, you say?*

Poppy: *Yes, rapper! And he's married to Kim Kardashian. Keep up!*

Me: *Kim who?*

Poppy: *Oh for God's sake! Kardashian! With the massive arse.*

(long pause)

Poppy: *You really don't know, do you?*

Me: *I'm afraid not.*

Poppy: *Have you been living under a rock for the last ten years?*

Me: *Of course not. But wasn't she at Glastonbury last year with her band?*

Poppy: *That was Kasabian!*

Me: *Is there a difference?*

Poppy: *I've got to go now…*

So, none the wiser then. But at least I've gleaned that this Kanye chap has a wife with a big bottom, which will surely hold me in good stead when I'm standing in a Somerset field, knee-deep in mud and surrounded by children who know who she is. What was it again? Kim something? I wonder if she's from North Korea.

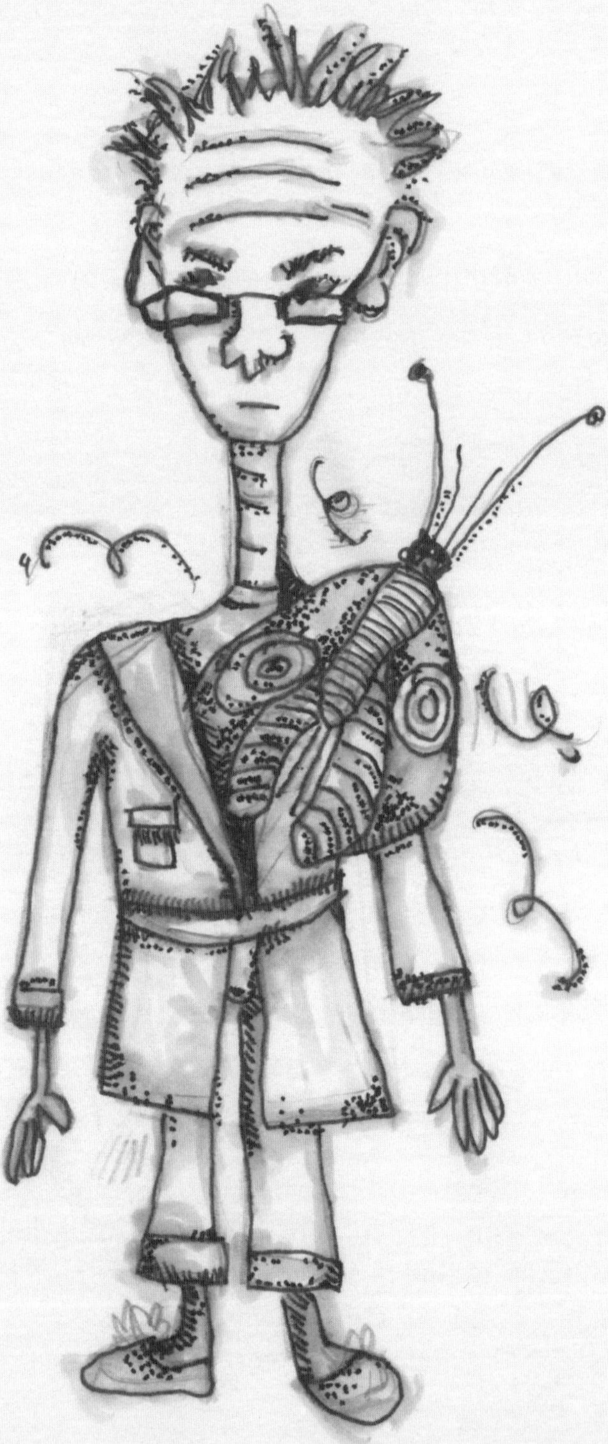

12

THE BEGINNING OF THE END

Another indicator that the writing is indeed on the wall.

ILLUSTRATION:
KETTA MORRIS

The Beginning of the End

A black moth shot out of my underpants as I was getting dressed this morning. Not in itself an event of huge import, but a salient reminder of the passing of thrusting alpha-manhood nonetheless. It must have been rather ancient, as presumably younger moths would frequent the undergarments of more potent individuals, those who would favour Abercrombie & Fitch and the like over the Heath Robinson-esque monstrosities I squeeze myself into every day. And this ageing Lepidoptera, exhausted from a lifetime of headbutting lightbulbs, would have given thanks to whatever god it believed in for this sedentary resting place, secure in the knowledge that it would remain undisturbed until its final day came. But it was not to be.

The symbolism of the moment was not lost on me: the moth is a portent of death. That, and that you don't do dry-cleaning enough. I was understandably perturbed (the very thought of having to waste a Saturday morning bagging up laundry was too ghastly to contemplate), but dealt with the issue in a manner fitting to anyone of a certain age familiar with micro-managing problems on a day-to-day basis: I forgot about it. But there is only so much evasion one can muster before the full weight of destiny crushes down hard upon the soul of a simpleton. That moth was telling me something, and that something I didn't want to know.

I leapt onto Facebook for some light relief, as is my wont in times of distress. And up there at the top of my feed was one of those irritating Suggested Posts, this one from the London Psychiatry Centre, suggesting I should do their wretched quiz to see if I was a one-in-four social pariah who drinks more than they recommend. Of course I was (the alternatives were patently absurd), and next thing I knew

I was getting a personal pledge from Dr Christos Kouimtsidis to help me on my journey towards a healthier lifestyle.

Now, I have never met Dr Kouimtsidis and, to be perfectly honest, am unlikely to any time soon. So it is doubtful I will get the opportunity to explain to him (through whichever slurred words he can understand), that the reason I am right up there on his critical list is because a moth has been residing in my pants for God knows how long, that my days left on Earth are clearly numbered and, this being the case, that I might choose to spend them cradling a bottle of something half-decent rather than being bored witless in a Harley Street waiting room. At prices that would secure the former by the pallet-load. Death, in whichever wondrous shape and form it has in store for me, will bloody well come when I so choose, Dr K. And now, if you don't mind, I'm off to the laundrette.

13

THE BLOOD TEST

Doctors are invariably hard as nails these days to keep you out of the surgeries. Dr Nunn was no different, particularly when I pointed out my fags were keeping him in work.

ILLUSTRATION:
DIGITAL PRIMATE

The Blood Test

In May 2013, I made an appointment with a certain Dr Nunn for a routine blood test. Apparently you're meant to do this sort of thing when the ratio of your years left on the planet versus years already used up, tips unfavourably towards the latter. I made light of any reasoning behind it, of course, suggesting that my request was purely investigative and of no great consequence. However, Dr Nunn is no fool. Looking straight past the saffron-tinted jellies through which I decipher the world and deep into the very core of my being, he offered me a seat next to the computer. Then he made me wait. For eons.

Time slows down to a crawl when you know you've been rumbled. The skinny document containing my records was theatrically scrutinised, and accusatory glances from over the top of his half-moon glasses were staged for maximum gravitas. I knew what was coming next:

Dr Nunn: *Smoker?*

Me: *Er… Not really. The occasional puff, perhaps.*

Dr Nunn: *How many?*

Me: *Hmm… Depends on my week, I suppose! (laughs nervously)*

Dr Nunn: *I'll put you down for twenty. Sound about right?*

Me: *Absolutely. (rapid blinking)*

Dr Nunn: *What about alcohol? How many units per week?*

Me: *Units? I'm not sure, to be honest. How do you…*

Dr Nunn: *Someone of your age should be looking at no more than one or two small glasses of wine a night. Preferably with breaks in-between. The liver isn't a miracle worker.*

Me: *I see. I think it would be fair to say I drink a little more than that. Not always, and I do try to keep it to…*

Dr Nunn: *I need a straight answer. Or we're both wasting each other's time, aren't we?*

Me: *Yes, I'm sorry. Well, on the odd occasion it has been known for me to get through half a bottle of red wine in the evening, and sometimes a beer or two.*

Dr Nunn: *How often? (long pause)*

Me: *Every night. (long pause)*

Dr Nunn: *No more than that? (long pause)*

Me: *No. (swallows)*

Dr Nunn: *Right, I need you to come back next week. Give this in at reception, they'll make another appointment for you.*

Me: *Thanks very much for…*

Dr Nunn: *Goodbye.*

I looked down at the printout thrust into my hand. There, in a little box marked *Relevant Clinical Details* was the evidence statisticians and the red tops pay top dollar for, no doubt to keep dipsomaniacs such as myself out of the surgeries. *Screen: high alcohol.* And it works. Because I never went back. If half a bottle of Pinot and a hop-based aperitif counts as alcohol abuse, my return visit would have seen Dr Nunn strapping me into some kind of detox seat, like Alex from *A Clockwork Orange*, forcing me to watch endless loops of waterfalls and Bavarian milkmaids until I recanted my feckless ways. Do me a favour.

14

THE SONG OF A SCEPTIC

I'm still waiting for the day when space pills become a thing.

ILLUSTRATION:
REBECCA PARKIN

The Song of a Sceptic

A little while back, I wrote a short piece about food on another platform when I was attempting to find my voice. It was deliberately confrontational and probably a touch derivative, the main thrust being that food is, in essence, merely petrol to keep us all alive in order to do far greater things than the act of eating itself. This would have been apposite if written in the 1970s (or indeed earlier), when the greater irony may well have been appreciated by frequenters of those unspeakable trattorias, nascent curry houses and stick-in-the-mud bastions of public school cuisine. But it wasn't.

Over the last twenty years or so, we have morphed into a nation of foodies. Suddenly, every man and his dog has developed a palate that subtle, it would leave Abigail and her guests floundering like jetsam at one of her soirées. We demand choice and quality as standard (despite having come through the worst recession since WW2) and, more than ever, we require affirmation that our opinions are justified. Why so?

Because our newfound appreciation of all things gastronomic is nothing more than the emperor's new clothes. We food snobs, like wine snobs, know deep down that our honed interest in comestibles is pretty low down on the pecking order of things that truly matter; consequently, in much the same way that our current government operates, we surround ourselves with like-minded sycophants who will be the first to forgive us for thinking that it does. So when the bill payer clicks his/her fingers at a chain restaurant minion and they come running, no one from either camp dares question the validity of the challenge. Money talks, deafeningly when there isn't much around, and putting an opinionated Herbert to rights is probably not worth losing your job for.

But it is a wafer-thin confidence, to be annihilated absolutely in the not too distant future by global events, the seething aficionados of packaged goods, and common sense. I predict a time when all celebrity chefs are dragged by the hair from their culinary idylls, thrown into the stocks and pelted to death with every last leaf of kale, lollo rosso and organically farmed, locally sourced cucumber that inevitably ended its days in the recycling bin. When coffee houses, like televisions in the 1950s, only offer black and white as an option, and if anyone with a manicured moustache demands anything with more than one syllable, they too will be executed on-site in the manner of Charles I and their remains fed to Hugh Fearnley-Whittingstall's pigs. And when the beasts of Smithfield, at the point of their bloody departure from this world to the restaurants of St John Street, are given the option to turn the tables, they do so on the sole condition that they feast exclusively on their perpetrators.

Ladies and gentlemen, I give you the future.

15

THE LURE OF THE LAND

There is no lure, trust me. It's tedious admin you have to get through until wine o'clock.

ILLUSTRATION:
TIM SIDDALL

The Lure of the Land

Buying the freehold of a property is usually one of those below the waterline affairs, a bit like getting the drains done or lancing the cat's boils; you sort of know it's the right thing to do, but there's scant instant gratification and every time you come away wondering why you bothered. It does seem frightfully grown-up, and when you mention it to grown-ups who've already done it, they all go to that grown-up place where grown-ups go when they've grown up and start throwing gibberish at you about longevity of leases and the like. Which only serves to confuse you further and makes you wish you'd blown it all on wine gums.

Pretty much anything to do with real estate is breathtakingly dull. From the fatuous language employed by conveyancing lawyers to justify their staggering fees, to the endless bureaucratic leeches waiting in line for their share of the silver, everything is precision-tailored to bore the pants off you and grind you into acquiescence. Even the figures bandied about at point of sale are so completely beyond your frame of reference, you find yourself internally knocking off a few noughts in order to make sense of them:

> **Lawyer:** *Thanks for coming in. Just to clarify – we have prepared and lodged a memorandum of transfer, checked for easements against existing title certificates, conducted relevant authority and chancel repair searches, discussed buildings insurance liabilities with current landlord, checked official copies and covenants relating to ongoing maintenance of common parts, and some other shit you wouldn't understand. If all the above is in order, we suggest a sum in advance of £50,000 would be appropriate for services rendered to date. Help yourself to a Freddo Frog on the way out.*

See? I mean, how do you respond? By the time you've worked out what the first half means to you, the layman, the suggested sum will have effectively doubled. Bizarrely, by taking the initial hit you're quids in. Which is why these SOBs remain gainfully employed and are always on holiday in the week of completion, whilst you are frantically checking the Land Registry for any long-forgotten relatives who may or may not own bits of Norfolk currently in tender to developers.

With the above in mind, I've been doing a bit of developing as well, and I don't mean pictures. What if, in the vein of that bloke Dave who set up his own bank, Idle Eye breaks the mould with a no-nonsense, one-stop shop for people who want to buy things without all that suffocating obfuscation? Hear me out:

You: *I'd like to buy this, please.*

Me: *Of course! It costs £x.*

You: *You have been most helpful. Here's a cheque.*

Me: *Thank you. I shall bank it forthwith. Enjoy your purchase.*

It's not hard. Really, it isn't. And who knows, it might even catch on. After all, there's an election coming up.

TYRELL

16

THE VOX MACHINA

I don't want to live well for less. I just want the patronising voices to shut up for five minutes when I'm shopping, and let me buy my 3 for 2 car starters in peace.

ILLUSTRATION:
SASCHA GRAVENSTEIN

The Vox Machina

Is it just me, or does every superstore these days feel the need to talk to its customers as if we have successfully navigated a maiden voyage to the lavatory without sullying the floor, or caking ourselves in our own oomska? If you're not sure what I'm on about here, pop over to your nearest supermarket of choice when you've read this. I can guarantee that within five minutes of entering the building, an intrusive announcement, broadcast to all by a Robson Green clone imitating Mick Jagger, will suggest you make a small diversion to the bakery aisle, where freshly-made, 3 for 2 doughnuts will help you live well. For less.

It's not the content that bothers me particularly though; it's the delivery. That sudden plunge, from innocuous mid-range to deeply offensive baritone, has been cynically calculated to recall in every shopper the halcyon days of their childhood, when Mummy would almost come if you managed to down a forkful of fish finger. This then triggers a rush of serotonin to the brain, and has us scurrying like insects towards whichever wretched product is currently on promotion, in order to keep the high going.

And it doesn't stop there. Why not punish yourselves further by putting in a quick call to your broadband provider? For the sheer hell of it! If and when you manage to get past the teenage cheerleader and her plethora of unfathomable options, you can enjoy Vivaldi's *Four Seasons* at tinnitus-inducing volume, until she starts banging on about the hash key should you fancy a few more. Has anyone ever done this? Actually opted for more options? The only reason to do so I can imagine is because you have been lured, as if by sirens, into a perpetual loop of doom, seduced by the prospect of discovering the magic key that will end your purgatory once and for all. At a premium call rate, naturally.

I know this makes me seem like a terrible Luddite. Or one of those grumpy old men you see on the telly who have already become versions of their own disdain. But hold up! If technology is as smart as they make out, why can't *we* get to choose the voice of whichever organisation is preaching at us? Based on preferences stored up there in the Cloud and fully configurable to suit our mood. All of a sudden, that dreaded Sunday excursion to Ikea doesn't seem so bad, does it? Just as you begin to glaze over in the BILLY bookcase department, Mariella Frostrup virtually detects your loss of will to live, and purrs something suggestive about meatballs into the headphones provided. And before you know it, you're making a beeline for the restaurant as your family struggles to keep up.

Not bad, eh? Maybe Apple should consider something along these lines when that watch of theirs comes out next month. And maybe then I'll consider a third doughnut.

HEINZ
Tomato
Soup

17

THE NEW KiDS

Utopian kitchens will be stocked with two items only: food and drink. Like in Repo Man. And that will be an end to the nonsense.

ILLUSTRATION:
SARAH EVANS

The New Kids

The heralding in of a new year traditionally allows the festivity-weary reveller to discard the old (a possible exception being the antiquities dealer), whilst simultaneously embracing all that is new, untried, untested and, to be frank, still in shorts. On this I beg to differ, particularly with regard to the contentious subject of foodstuffs. The last couple of weeks have seen all manner of pretenders cross the threshold, charge up the stairs and vie for pole position in a kitchen already bulging with the decomposing diehards of previous months, quietly biding their time with patience, good grace and a certain dignity. The futility of their plight is not lost on me and my heart goes out to them.

For example, a brattish bunch of dates muscled their way in the other day, flashing their knickers from inside a Taste the Difference box. And, not content with their star placement in front of the wine emporium, they demanded to be addressed as MEDJOOL DATES, all vulgar capitals and a Best Before sticker that had the longer-term residents wincing. The bravado of the wretched things was beyond belief, particularly as, on closer inspection, they bore a strong resemblance to a miserable collection of sun-dried testicles in captivity. I note wryly as I write this that they remain unopened and have started sucking up to the shallots.

Then there is the issue of the cheese cracker. For years, we have been content with the only after-dinner companion wafer that has ever mattered – the Carr's Table Water Biscuit. Fashioned in Carlisle for quality and durability, the CTWB has more than proven its worth and has no need at all to jump about in fancy packaging. In fact, the bland blue/black box instils in us a sense of consumer confidence the new kids can only dream of. But still they come: Thomas J Fudge (with his faux-Victorian offerings and endless chummy waffle); the more austere Fine English Cheese Co., (who put on a good show but are ultimately undone by a packshot of the product, gasping for breath from beneath a gargantuan slab of Red Leicester) and many, many more, too risible to mention here.

What these culinary contenders for the kitchen throne seem to have forgotten (or are simply too naive to comprehend) is that their time will also come, and the bitter pill they shall be forced to swallow is that of humility. Either that, or suffer the slings and arrows of the green bin which will be only too happy to see them out. For there is no more tragic a sight than seasonal goods preening themselves like they're the cat's pyjamas when everyone else in the room can see them for what they are: has-beens, like ex-footballers with a boutique restaurant or ex-rockers with a ponytail. So, in light of the above, my lunch today will come from a tin containing one of 57 varieties. It's my small way of saying thanks for being right there at the back. Going nowhere.

18

THE SMEAR

My latest rodent-based conspiracy theory. Really must stop doing this.

ILLUSTRATION:
TIM FERGUSON

The Smear

Eagle-eyed readers will have spotted that the humble gerbil has graced the dailies once again, but not in a good way. Turns out our furry brethren can no longer be considered impossibly cute playthings of the very young (and, on occasion, my good self), being as they are conveyors of misery, disease and quality herbs and spices brought in on the Silk Road. And we're also expected to believe that in 1347, in between exercising on their little wooden wheels and nibbling whatever they liked nibbling back in medieval Syria, they found time to pop over to London and give us all the Black Death.

It is a monstrous slur, cooked up by some Norwegian boffin with too much time on his hands, and fails to digest some pretty basic facts. For starters, there is no evidence whatsoever that gerbils took up residence in the UK until comparatively recently. Why would they? If your thing is copious quantities of sand and sunshine, you'd probably give it a bit of a wide berth. Not to mention the logistical issues if and when you finally made it to Calais. Absolute nonsense!

Furthermore, architectural clues only date back to the 1950s. Before Rotastak – the Nottingham-based pioneers of affordable rodent housing – there were slim pickings to be had if you were small, hirsute and over here. Rats understood this unconditionally, so they made alternative arrangements. But they were also robust and greasy enough to hack it. Their smaller, more delicate cousins wouldn't have lasted five minutes. You can take Syria out of the gerbil etc…

Clearly we are being whipped up into a collective state of anxiety. It's what the media does when it wants us to go to war, or sanction the spending of taxpayer cash on something unpalatable the government has shares in. What on earth can the gerbil have done to get them wound up so? And why are we being told that the more sinister rat is the fall guy? It smacks of Andy and Rebekah, the former taking the hit so the latter can persist with her satanic craft. Something stinks up there in the corridors of power, but what?

And then it struck me. Helen Perley's exquisite 32-page tome *Enjoy Your Gerbil* (The Pet Library™, 1971) clearly states that the same is no ordinary rodent, and frequently refers to him as a 'superpet'. Probably the exact kind of pet that could radicalise British teenage girls into making the arduous pilgrimage to his homeland. And guess where that is? See? By demonising the critters, we surreptitiously put the brakes on the next wave of IS recruits and no one gets hurt. No one, that is, except these innocents abroad, and who speaks for them? Who will fight their corner after the first spate of distressing pet murders? And which sick individual will be the first to expand their perspex property portfolio at the expense of the less fortunate?

Right there.

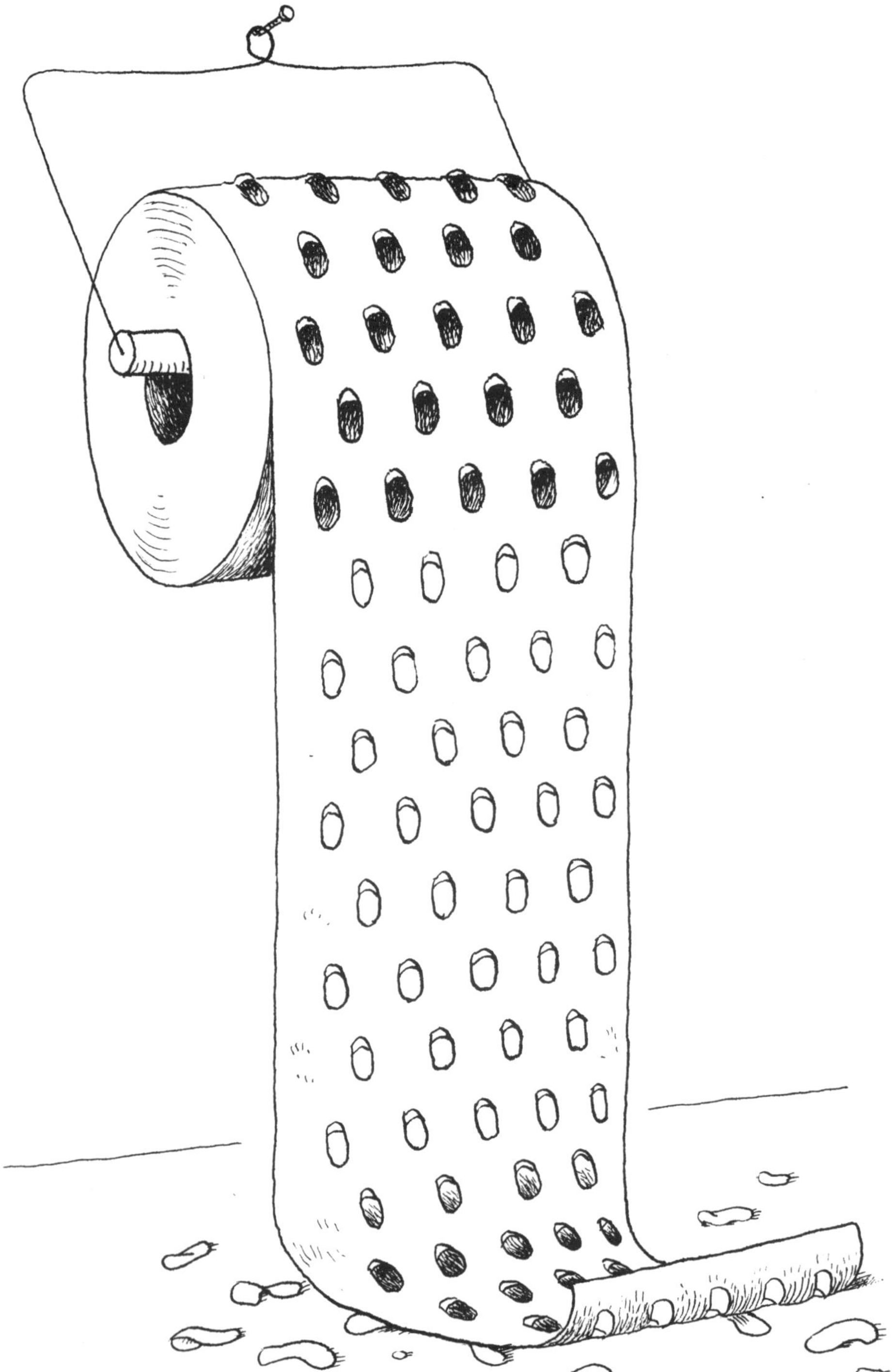
MARK

19

THE BiG TiSSUE

I've never quite understood the concept of quilting, as if some bottoms are born greater than others. The small room is one of the very few places in which we are all truly equal.

ILLUSTRATION:
MARK WEIGHTON

The Big Tissue

Has anyone noticed that toilet roll tubes are shrinking? Anyone? I've been giving this one some thought of late (as the former owner of thirteen gerbils, my attention to such matters is a tad more devout than you might otherwise think) and I cannot for the life of me imagine why. You reduce the circumference of the tube, ergo the volume of tissue necessary to fill the gap increases. And surely it is more cost-effective to expand the cardboard by an insignificant fraction than to manufacture the extra sheets? Not to mention of all that extra perforating and, if you're posh, quilting. We've all got used to the stealth techniques employed by supermarkets and the like with their swingeing reduction in product proportion, but this is blatantly a false economy and somebody's head should roll.

Then there's the matter of quality. Does anyone remember when you only needed a couple of sheets to wipe the slate clean? Because they were the thickness of a small sandwich or a baby's mattress? Or how about Izal medicated, the robust choice of municipal buildings, schools and the more progressive public conveniences? So hardy was it, in fact, it could stop a Sherman tank in full flight if lined up correctly. Well, without putting too fine a point on it, nowadays you could copy the entire works of Charles Dickens onto the paper necessary for just one go. And the end user (oh stop it!) lives in permanent fear of finger pop. Don't think we haven't noticed, Mr Andrex! And no amount of impregnated aloe vera is gonna make up for all that chafing.

But fear not, my friends. I put in yet another narratively convenient call to Nibs* earlier and he assures me that the exceptional tissue provided by the Idle Hour has maintained its AAA status for another year. And, as one of the lucky few who has stood sheet to cheek in the traps, I can vouch for the same. These bountiful beauties are organic, responsibly sourced, line-caught and hand-stitched by vestal virgins at the foothills of the Appenines for your sanitary convenience. No horse DNA, no artificial sweeteners, no CFCs, no nonsense. And a free drink at the bar if you can punch a hole through the middle. Pre-application, obviously.

Finally, a word to the ladies from Nibs himself. Apparently, you lot are whipping through the stuff like it's going out of fashion, and, being a gentleman of good character, he is loath to drop by and investigate. Vast, industrial-strength tubes regularly vanish into thin air, and whilst he is aware that there are many bottoms to feed, demand is seriously outstripping supply. May I suggest that you 'make room' before you leave the house? We are living through a time of unprecedented austerity and it's only fair that you do your bit. And us blokes promise to wipe up the oversplash when we get in. Right, lads?

*My brother, owner of the Idle Hour pub and my former employer.

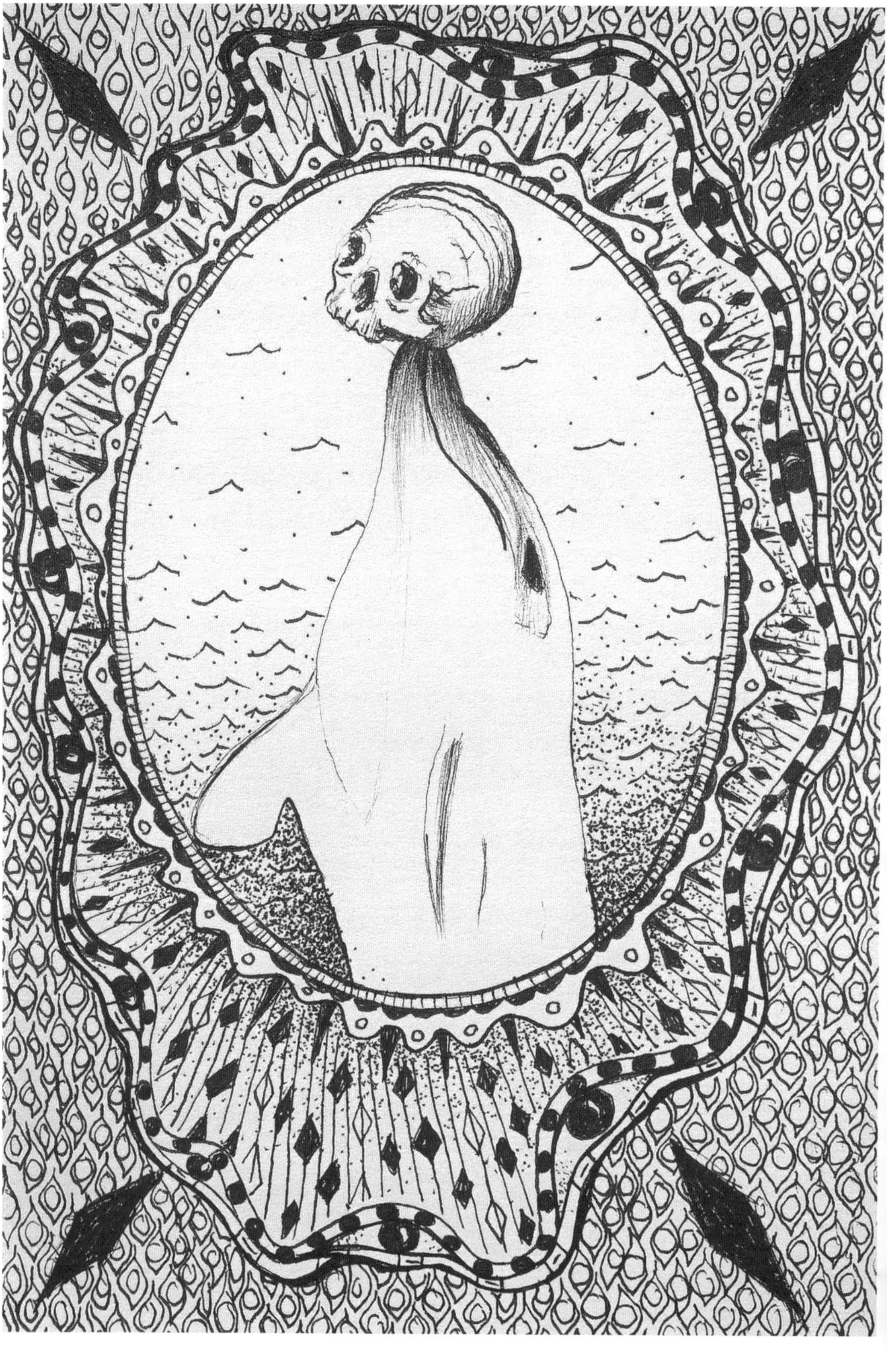

20

THE STATE OF DENMARK

I was being deliberately cryptic here. There was stuff I needed to get off my chest but couldn't, so I threw up this faux pomp instead. Still not telling, mind.

ILLUSTRATION:
MARK DICEY

The State of Denmark

Good title. Well, I like it. Those of you who had your Coriolanuses kicked into reading the Bard's greater works at school will recognise that the broader idiom suggests an element of brooding malcontent; that something in the land of salty liquorice is not exactly as it should be. See, you're already hooked! Perhaps one of the perilously thin strands along which we all conduct our lives has become tangled or broken. Perhaps a moral compass has been thrown out of kilter. Perhaps it's all an elaborate decoy to throw you off the scent. Perhaps, perhaps, perhaps, as our Doris once succinctly put it.

As I write this, it is the hottest day the UK has cooked up in a decade. And heat, as I'm sure you're aware, plays havoc with the brain and those last remaining pollutants of Glastonbury. The synapses within sizzle and fuse, neurons struggle to function and the propensity for rational thought gradually deliquesces into chaos and confusion. So what chance does one have if this is the moment to step up to the plate? To make brave, life-altering decisions before yielding to the charms of high summer and going out topless into the streets (the Englishman at home's favourite pastime)? It's a one word answer – fat.

In that tragic-heroic fashion all romantic schoolboys are prone to, I was once asked (after midnight, around a flickering tealight) to declare the one thing I'd be prepared to give up everything else for. And, being a relatively inexperienced resident on our complex planet, I answered, with some certainty, that it would be the aquamarine pair of Speedos (with white printed dolphins bobbing their merry way across my privates) I had just been given for Christmas. I was serious. Life had not yet complicated my childish aspirations, and I could think of nothing or no one I wanted more. And in some ways, it was the perfect response. Perfect in its unswerving simplicity, and perfect because it was a need easily fulfilled. No hopes dashed, no hearts broken. And it would probably be different the next day. Ironically, it was the summer of '76. Another hot one.

Then we age. And as we march through our lives, things get increasingly difficult. They just do. We steal moments of pleasure wherever we can, in the full knowledge that they will probably be fleeting and outweighed by the sheer pressure of hanging in there. It's why our occupations are so much more than a means to an end. They define us. They validate the reasons for our being alive at all. Otherwise we're merely grown-up sperm looking for something to do. If asked the same question again, after all this time, I only wish the answer could be as economic. But the things we crave in later life inevitably come at a price, by which I do not mean anything so vulgar as money. And we're usually too busy to notice.

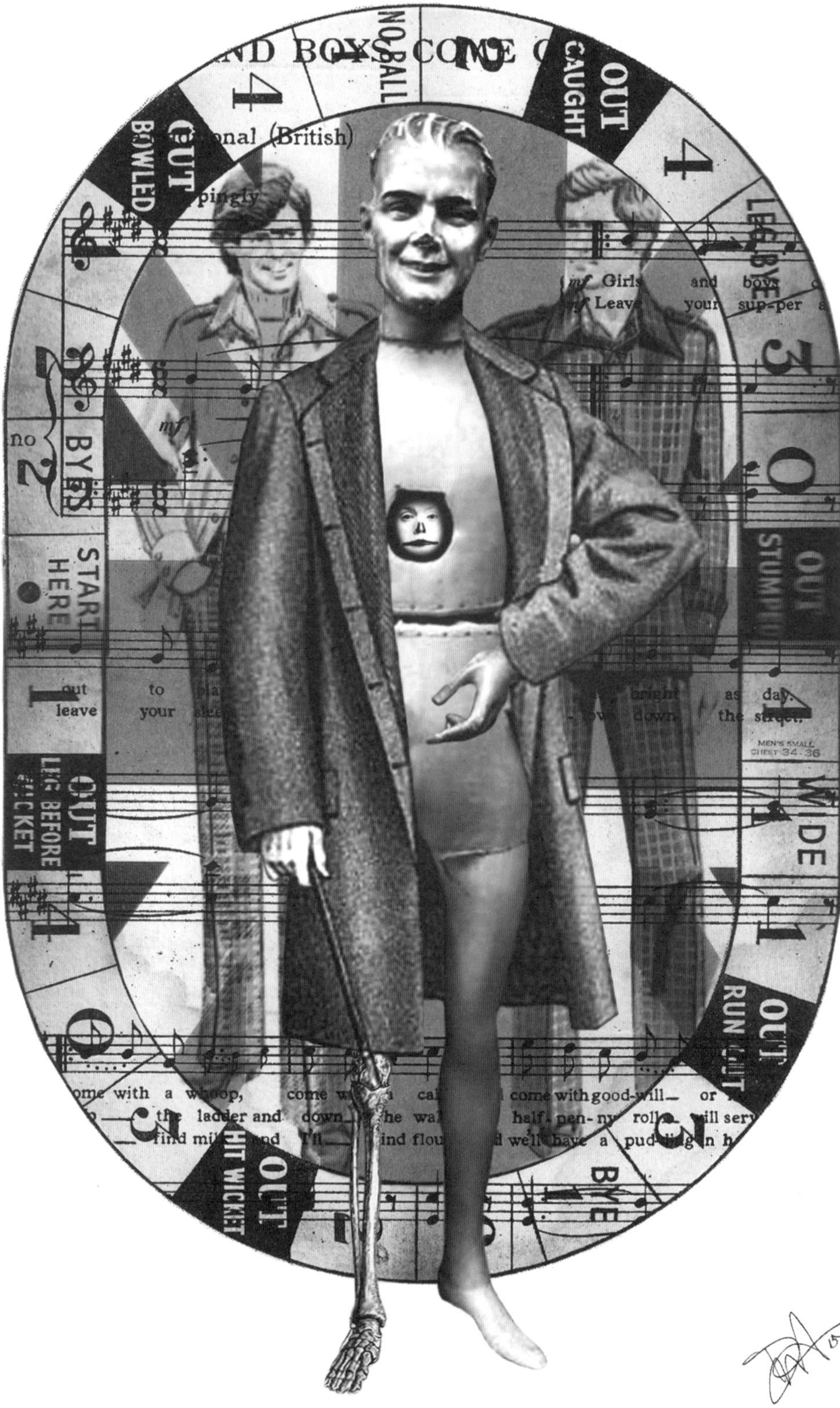

NO BALL
OUT CAUGHT
OUT BOWLED
onal (British)
Girls and boys
Leave your sup-per
BYES
START HERE
leave your
bright as day.
down the street.
MEN'S SMALL CHEST 34-36
WIDE
OUT RUN OUT
come with a whoop,
come with good-will
the ladder and
half-pen-ny roll
OUT HIT WICKET
BYE

21

THE RAG TRADE-OFF

Hanging onto old clothes is supposedly an early warning sign that you have issues. I rest my case.

ILLUSTRATION:
THE DNA FACTORY

The Rag Trade-Off

Like most males of my age, I'm an uncomfortable clothes shopper. The very idea of leaving the cosy womb of my flat, for a strip-lit warehouse touting whichever offensive garment happens to be fashionable right now, is so distressing that I tend to hang onto the same tatty old shite, attempting to cover my nakedness for one more glorious season rather than face the alternative. I'm not proud of it, but that's the truth. And as every summer leaves what autumn finds, I have learned to recognise that 50/50 mix of pity and disgust buried deep beneath the permafrost of those I hold dearest. They try to disguise it, bless 'em, but I know it's there. And it hurts because I know they know I only have two sartorial settings: Dress to Impress, and Dress Down Weekday.

Take, for instance, my Bolongaro Trevor 'God Save the King' tee shirt with its attendant heraldic symbols, furry-faced monarchs in period ellipse frames and mottled serif type. This fits neatly into the former category and gets outed whenever I need to shine – about twice a decade. Anyone who witnessed the annihilation of popular song executed by my brother and I at the Idle Hour last year may have spotted it. My fervent prayer was that you'd be so impressed by the packaging, a closer inspection of the contents would have been unnecessary. And while we're on the subject, could someone have a word with him about that Union Jack jacket? We all know it's a magnificent beast but there's a fine line between Mo Farah and Jimmy Savile.

In the latter corner lies my John Lewis knee-length overcoat. This loyal lovely has been doing the rounds since the Boer War and was dyed black in 1926 in order to disguise the blood of fallen suffragettes and rotting stitches stolen from a roadside hospital in Ypres. If it were a tree it would be a Douglas Fir – solid, dependable and stoic.

A bit like Jeremy Clarkson. The inside pockets, however, have frayed beyond repair (although this does have the advantage of easy access to my person for those essential 'on the road' adjustments).

Also worth mentioning are the unmentionables. Yes, it's those grey 2003 boulder holders I never thought would last more than a few months, but like the Council Tax and Tesco Metro have managed to survive despite multilateral resentment. Admittedly there's not much to fall in love with here, but as the years have gone by, they have formed an impressive crust on the inside elastic which has aided and abetted adhesion to the waistline. Sorry ladies, he's taken.

They say charity begins at home. And I have a bag marked the same which will never, never see a shop marked the same. Because there's always a couple more years left. At *least* a couple.

22

THE PIG'S TABLE

Boarding schools in the '70s were brutal. To survive unscathed, you pretty much had to be feral. And God help you if you were claimed by the 'Table'.

ILLUSTRATION:
URSULA MCLAUGHLIN

The Pig's Table

The 1970s. A decade of strikes, skyrocketing inflation, shocking trousers, way too much hair and cars that didn't start in the morning. But to this then knock-kneed schoolboy with nascent food issues and a paranoic fear of authority, it will forever be remembered as the one that threw up the Pig's Table. And I mean that quite literally. Let me get you up to speed.

The PT was an abominable form of ritual humiliation, cooked up by some of the sickest minds this side of the Nuremberg trials and callously administered by a stringent headmistress and the minions in her employ. These punitive cronies were known collectively as The Danes, whose *raison d'être* was to concoct a regular school meal that could be instantaneously jettisoned by any formative digestive system within a fifty foot radius. In this they were ruthlessly efficient. The universally feared Egg Nest™ – an impossibly thick substrate of aqueous grey potato cunningly concealed beneath a quagmire of zygotic discharge – was the jewel in their crown. Even Heston has not yet superseded this terrifying Frankendish, and God knows he's tried.

In the days before CCTV, food slop bins were manned in shifts. The trick was to get your plate of Egg Nest™ in there at point of changeover and make a break for the door before the new guard had worked out what was going on. But alas, as many did try, so many more failed and were instantly fed into the sausage machine of corrective punishment. First, a guilt-inducing rebuke: how that the thousands, if not millions of disadvantaged children in some of our poorest nations would be pathetically grateful for the delicacy you had just rejected. At which point you resisted the urge to mention Parcel Post. But then came the killer. Your penance would be exacted the very next day. You would suffer the Table.

I'll take you through it. Like Spartacus, albeit unshackled, you were led into the refectory, filled to capacity with one hundred plus Lords of the Flies with an immense thirst for cruelty, and thrust towards a table for one. This braying throng, despite having narrowly missed the margin themselves, saw you as legitimate quarry and mocked mercilessly as you took your seat, steeling yourself for the imminent arrival of yesterday's Egg Nest™. When it turned up, more congealed and pitiful than before, so began the painfully slow process of its consumption. The concurrent gagging was met with a wall of prepubescent ridicule, sweat, bile and fear meshing together as one as you prayed to whichever deity was in the vicinity to make it all stop.

It did eventually. But as you collected your thoughts in the ensuing nauseous aftermath, you knew you'd never be the same again. You had become a husk, a grotesque traumatised ghost of your former self, and mealtimes would from now on be heinous culinary skirmishes for you to fight and lose.

So, lunch anyone?

23

THE LADYGRAPE OF WRATH

Samantha has since become a firm friend.
I'll miss her when she's gone.

ILLUSTRATION:
ANTHONY REYNOLDS

The Ladygrape of Wrath

Wrestling myself into consciousness on Saturday morning I noticed, right there in the bed beside me, a bump I didn't recall inviting back the night before. It had not been a dramatic Friday, for I'd only had a quick pizza with my friend Donald before making it home without a statutory flying visit to Wetherspoons. I did briefly consider waking it and offering it a cup of coffee until I discovered, to my escalating distress, that indeed, my guest had not muscled its way in after an ill-advised drinking session, but was comfortably attached to my person. And as if that wasn't harrowing enough, to an area not traditionally associated with the finer points of romance.

A more intimate inspection was clearly requisite, one that involved my shaving mirror and a rudimentary attempt at yoga. And there, as in one of those early Victorian birthing daguerreotypes, was a minuscule extension of myself, nestled deep within the nucleus of an unattractive forest of hair and flesh. It was approximately the size of a hazelnut and seemed perfectly at ease with its newfound location, to the extent that it made me feel like a low-rent Henry Morton Stanley having just stumbled upon Dr Livingstone. I almost apologised for disturbing it.

Several online diagnoses later brought me to the unhappy conclusion that I was going to have to radically alter my diet, drink less Pinot and more water, do exercise and shower every five minutes just to appease the little bastard. For this was to be no symbiotic arrangement, at least as far as I could tell, which pissed me off. And as its correct medical moniker was way too long and disgusting for me to use on a regular basis, I decided to call it Samantha by way of softening the blow. In retaliation for this perceived slight, she made it nigh-on impossible for me to sit down for three days.

Unless I'm steaming, I've never been particularly accomplished at making new acquaintances. I tend to linger behind the protective cloak of shyness until somebody else makes the first move. The doctor at my GPs, however, was unfettered by any such inhibitions. She and Samantha got on famously, gossiping away as if they were entrenched in a nightclub lavatory and had known each other for years. I lay on my side, facing the acid green wall with my knees pressed up against my ears and wondered at which stage of the appointment they might notice I was still present. After they'd exchanged phone numbers, I was told that Samantha and I would have to learn to get along, and turfed out into the rain.

Thank the Lord, she's eased off a bit on the searing pain. But frankly, I'm getting sick of having to make all the effort. If she were a flatmate, I'd have words. But she's not. She's a thrombosed external haemorrhoid. Try telling that to your mates and staying fashionable, bitch.

24

THE TALENTED MR REYNARD

London is full of foxes. They don't even try to hide these days and we've all got kind of used to them. Except, true to form, the press continues to stoke our base fears with vile scare stories, so someone had to speak up in their defence. Ahem.

ILLUSTRATION:
CLAIRE FLETCHER

The Talented Mr Reynard

I was making my regular journey to the train earlier today when something stopped me in my tracks. And before you get unnecessary, it wasn't the sciatica or any other dreary ailment that prohibits the fluid motion of youth. No, this was far more interesting: on the pavement, not one hundred yards from my flat, lay a vast pile of fox business. Not, as you might imagine, lying there passively like a collection of ancient churros. Far from it. These were super-fresh and neatly stacked, resembling a miniature log rick to be used at a future date for some demonic purpose or other. And it got me to thinking that your fox has evolved in ways that couldn't have been imagined when I was a kid. Back then, they were timid, seldom-seen creatures that you might occasionally catch a fleeting glimpse of when you visited your nan in the countryside. Not any more: his urban cousin has got streetwise, people-savvy and bold as brass. And we love him for it.

Let me give you an example: earlier this year, the evergreen *Daily Mail* ran the story of Tod, a fox who got barred from his local pub in Beverley, East Yorkshire. Impressive, huh? I only wish I could have seen his tab. But the naysayers all came from the 'vermin' camp, and consequently poor Tod was prevented from enjoying what was rightfully his after a long day of wrestling pizzas from parochial wheelie bins. And the delightful *sickofthiscountry* was so righteously indignant that such a wretch wasn't properly toilet-trained, she almost dropped one of her own off online.

Now, I know this might upset some of you country folk, but London is furry friendly. Yep, all disease-ridden social pariahs can pop over any time they like and down a pint or two in their own good time. And the foxes are welcome as well. Oh, and anyone who has a problem with this can take it up with me outside. Just because we city types don't have an arsenal of profitable livestock to protect, doesn't mean we can't extend common courtesy to strangers; otherwise you other lot, Dubrovnik Dave and Sarajevo Steve, can swing for it. Them's the rules these days. And while we're at it, instead of getting all Theresa May about our shaggy brethren, how about we capitalise on their inherent skillset and integrate it into our own? Imagine the possibilities.

Sly, highly-motivated worker required for hen house security position. Must be slim, hairy and hated by the right-wing press. Penchant for sleeping infants a bonus, as is the ability to create a pyramid of turd just wherever. Enjoys running, fast food, medieval fables, Yorkshire bitter and squealing after midnight like a girl. Rates negotiable. Start when we've mended the French doors.

Message? What we fear is not necessarily the enemy. And put your bloody rubbish in a bin.

25

THE CHRISTMAS SPECIAL

I love Desert Island Discs. The best bit is working out whether the featured guest is bullshitting or genuinely enjoying their selections. Kirsty is the consummate professional, regardless. This was my take on being at the business end.

ILLUSTRATION:
MAGDA ARCHER

The Christmas Special

Desert Island Discs – December 2014

Kirsty: *Due to swingeing cuts the BBC has suffered recently, my castaway this week is alcoholic and sometime blogger Idle Eye. I know, me neither. His pithy and often self-deprecating blog has been read by an ever-decreasing audience since its inception in 2011, and he claims to be a mouthpiece for the very few disaffected, middle-aged misanthropes he manages to connect with. Good morning, sir.*

Me: *Good morning, Kirsty.*

Kirsty: *I understand that you no longer make any money at all from your work. Is this true?*

Me: *That's correct. I started by writing for my brother's pub, but it soon became pretty clear that the drivel I put out was having an adverse effect on his clientele. They stayed away in their droves. The rest is history.*

Kirsty: *So what's the incentive, if you don't mind me asking?*

Me: *Well, Kirsty, the strapline for the whole shebang is 'getting it off my chest and onto yours', which I suppose is the main thrust. And I nicked that from Peter Cook. Unfortunately, there isn't an original bone in my body. But I soldier on.*

Kirsty: *Let's have some music.*

Me: *My first would have to be Instant Street by dEUS, which hit me like a bullet when it came out in 19…*

Kirsty: *We don't have that one, I'm afraid.*

Me: *Oh… Well, how about Heavenly Pop Hit by The Chills? The flagship band from New Zealand's Flying Nun stable when they were at their…*

Kirsty: *Nor that.*

Me: *I thought you had these things lined up beforehand?*

Kirsty: *Look, Sarah Millican asked for Wham! if that's any help. Work with me.*

Me: *OK.*

[You Drive Me Crazy – Shakin' Stevens]

Kirsty: *Thank you. Now, tell me about your drinking. You profess a disturbing reliance on Marlborough Pinot Noir in order to get your ideas onto the page. Would you describe yourself as a writer with a drinking problem, or a drinker with a writing problem?*

Me: *I like to think of it as both. Although it's clear which one would have to go if push came to shove.*

Kirsty: *I see. And do you think you could manage without?*

Me: *There's a lot of crap out there, Kirsty. And the telly's getting better and better. So yes, I think so.*

Kirsty: *Let's have your next disc.*

Me: *Can I have…*

[We Are The Champions – Queen]

Kirsty: *You mention your family in several posts. Tell me about the early years: did they spot the signs of your forthcoming invisibility or was it something you had to work at alone?*

Me: *When you say 'forthcoming invisibility'…*

Kirsty *That, by your own admission, your efforts are widely ignored. 'Like farting into a wind tunnel', as you once put it.*

Me: *It was a mutually beneficial arrangement, I seem to remember. To have your 'efforts' overlooked as a young man does stand you in good stead for later life. In many ways it was a gift, for which I am profoundly grateful.*

Kirsty: *Forgive me for bringing this up, but we're running out of time and we need a hook. Your father, a much-loved television and film actor, died last year. How did his tangible success, first realised when he was less than half your age, affect your confidence as an artist in your own right?*

Me: *Well Kirsty, I see it like this. Success is very much like wine: some of it can be enjoyed young (and some of it can be very good), but I think most of us would agree that in order for it to be at its very best, it needs to have sat around for a while.*

Kirsty: *But if you leave it too long, it gets tipped down the sink.*

Me: *There is that.*

Kirsty: *Let's have some more mu… Actually, let me do it.*

[Do They Know It's Christmas? – Band Aid]

Me: *I hate that one, by the way.*

Kirsty: *Me too. But it's your show.*

Me: *And I normally write 500 words, preferably less.*

Kirsty: *Say it's a Christmas special, you can do whatever you like with them. Now, I'm going to give you The Complete Works of Shakespeare and The Bible to take with you. And a book of your choice. What's it going to be?*

Me: *Well, it's a toss-up between...*

[Sarah Millican's Support Group audiobook – Sarah Millican (signed)]

Kirsty: *And a luxury too. You can have one thing on the island to make life more bearable.*

Me: *I'd like...*

[You're Never Too Fat For A Handbag – Sarah Millican white cotton tea towel (signed)]

Kirsty: *And if you had to pick just one... Ach, forget it.*

Me: *I already have.*

Kirsty: *Thanks for coming in.*

Me: *No, thank you.*

26

THE NEW SUITS OF BEDTIME

Apparently, a good pyjama says more about the person inside than money ever can. Which is handy, seeing as I haven't got any. But I do have an immaculate set of PJs which I try not to piss into on a daily basis.

ILLUSTRATION:
NICK HOLLYWOOD

The New Suits of Bedtime

I was down the pub on Monday with a trio of men of a certain age and, in amongst the plethora of tripe discussed, the subject of nightwear was gingerly raised. Obvs I plumped for the pyjama, but regrettably was riotously trashed at the post in favour of going commando, something I must confess I find rather disturbing in one's advancing years. All that naked flesh frotting away against raw cotton (or Crimplene – I do not judge) can not in any way be conducive to a good night's sleep. Let alone the potential for impure thought or any derivative thereof. The filth and the fury, the filth and the fury.

No, it's the pyjama every time in my book. The fact that they are restrictive is ironically at the very core of their genius. By wearing the things, we willingly shackle ourselves to such laudable traits as propriety, comfort and hygiene. And I'll go you one further – it is no accident they have matching tops and bottoms. Move over, city slickers! These are the new suits of bedtime, and ones we can all wear with pride and dignity at a fraction of the cost of their daytime equivalent. They are truly the egalitarian attire of our age.

I'm not saying they're for everyone. There is a certain build of man that insists on the elasticated waistband, a less refined beast one could not wish to see, let alone wear, despite its obvious practical advantages. Fortunately, modern manufacturers have taken this on board and come up with the button fly/drawstring combo. This cute little trick at once gets you out of the shit whilst somehow keeping you fashionable. And, more importantly perhaps, avoiding the phenomenon that is 'Ankle Island', an exposed wasteland no man beyond his fortieth year should ever have the misfortune to frequent. I take my hat off to these people. Only my hat.

To drive the point home, I purchased a classic striped PJ set from an expensive Chelsea retailer on my way home the very next day. Not for one moment that I imagined my friends would catch a glimpse of me gliding around my bedroom in those generously cut trousers with their two side pockets, or the timeless jacket with its full 5oz of cotton flannel. No, no, no! The exquisite pleasure gained here is not for sharing, which may explain why there is a paucity of targeted marketing on your social media. Access to such hallowed portals comes either by word of mouth, or from those bizarre mini-catalogues that drop out of the subscriber magazines. You know, the ones from which it is possible to buy salmon pink corduroys or a watch which apparently you don't own, despite having shelled out twenty grand for it. The beauty of a quality pyjama can only be genuinely appreciated by the man inside.

Tonight, and for the foreseeable future, I am that man.

Steady. Steady.
Just one more second...
EYE
DEPT

PSI
MIN
MAX
BUM
DEPT

27

THE ENEMY WITHIN

Shades of Das Boot. The sheer volume of gunk your body can chuck up when you're sick defies all logic. Until you read this.

ILLUSTRATION:
DAN LAIDLER

The Enemy Within

For the last 48 hours, I've been at war. However placid I may be in my natural state, when invaded by germs hell-bent on turning my internals into that green goo from *Dr Who*, I tend to kick off. For a while there, it looked as if they had the upper hand. First, they came for my voice, next for my nose and lungs and then, while I was rushing about tending to these, they came for my bottom. However, what they hadn't banked on was my British resilience in the face of extreme adversity. That, like any great military strategist, I could and would play the long game, feigning weakness and ineptitude when, in fact, I was building up to a mighty show of strength which would conclusively put them to rout. Something like this:

Germ A: *He's going into the bathroom, men! Weakest to the fore! WEAKEST TO THE FORE!!!*

Germ B: *It's OK, sir! He's only having a huey in the sink. No great loss.*

Germ A: *Right, get a message over to Nasal Production without delay. We're going for a massive push in ten.*

Germ B: *He's got some loo rolls by the bed, we'll be toast in seconds! If Bottom Bay gets cracking now, we stand more of a chance of catching him off guard when he goes back in.*

Germ A: *How many rolls?*

Germ B: *Not sure, sir. Maybe we should send a few privates up to the throat? They can have a quick butcher's when he's bent over the khazi.*

Germ A: *Too risky. We're down on mucus and we'll need everything we have for when he starts necking the Benylin.*

Germ B: *Benylin, sir?*

Germ A: *Yes, bloody Benylin! It was on the sideboard.*

Germ B: *That changes the rules a bit. How long do you think we have?*

Germ A: *Long enough to play merry hell with his bottom. Now get on with it!*

Germ B: *Germ B to Bottom Bay, Germ B to Bottom Bay, open all sluice gates now. I repeat, open sluice gates now!*

Bottom Bay: *Bottom Bay to Germ B, Bottom Bay to Germ B. We have a problem. The gates are wide but nothing's coming out. Urgently request reinforcements from Chest and/or Throat Depts. She's dry as a witch's tit, sir!*

Germ B: MAYDAY! MAYDAY! ALL MUCUS ZONES TO PROCEED TO BOTTOM BAY AT ONCE. THIS IS AN EMERGENCY! DO NOT HANG ABOUT!

Germ A: *He's got quilted! Bail out now!*

Germ B: *Too late. I've instructed all departments to head south.*

Germ A: *Oh my God, it's done. He was too good for us this time. Give my regards to your wife and family and should we survive, a swift drink at the Criterion when it's all over?*

Germ B: *Thank you. May I say it was an honour to serve under you?*

Germ A: *You may. Goodbye, B.*

Germ B: *Goodbye, sir.*

28

THE INSOMNIAC

I had six weeks of insomnia over the summer. Awful. Like the worst drug available to humanity, I didn't want it there and I didn't want it then. Or ever again, for that matter.

ILLUSTRATION:
MATT JEFFS

The Insomniac

There was a time I thought it impossibly cool to be able survive on little or no sleep; that I could glide, ghostlike, into the dark portals of my home over the small hours, content in the knowledge that lightweight recumbents lacking the requisite stamina could not manage the same. In much the same way as an ASBO, it was a badge of pride which would undoubtedly be the envy of the idle. So at the beginning of this book campaign, when I was riding high on nervous energy, I welcomed it in. '*Brilliant*', I thought, '*I'll coast through the jobs and come out ahead of the game*'. I could not have been more wrong. You know something's up when the crying kicks in:

– *Postman delivers wine stain remover? Howl like a baby.*
– *Blurry online photo of Cecil the Lion? Howl like a baby.*
– *Builders below stop using circular saw for twenty seconds? Howl like a baby.*

And that's only the beginning. Next up comes the attention deficit, always handy when you're multitasking:

Boil kettle / half complete to-do list / prepare for shower / remember kettle / make coffee half-dressed / ditto three lines of email / have shower / call someone / walk around park to clear head / remember email / check Facebook / quick cry / more coffee / check to-do list again / remember food / forget food / remember email / quick cry / go to bed.

The cruellest twist of the knife is that last bit. When you finally head up the hill, exhausted beyond language from your day of not quite achieving anything and discovering twenty different ways that sleep deprivation will see you off, you collapse into the welcoming haven of the bedroom. But it is a Trojan horse. Come stupid o'clock (usually ten to something ridiculous like two or three), you find yourself bolt upright and worrying about that bloody email. So now there's nul chance of getting back to Nod, yet somehow you have to fill up your time until the whole palaver starts all over again. And that's when the chatting starts:

Me: *Not sure how much more of this I can take.*

Me: *Me neither. It's savage.*

Me: *Sure is. What shall we do?*

Me: *Think anyone's on Messenger?*

Me: *Doubt it. How about a bit of Facebook stalking?*

Me: *Yeah, why not?*

(Two minutes later)

Me: *Sod this. Let's go for a walk.*

Me: *Too knackered.*

Me: *Book then?*

Me: *We'll end up reading the same sentence again and again. Like last night.*

Me: *Smoke?*

Me: *Yeah, that's going to help.*

Me: *Well what do you suggest then, smartarse?*

Me: *How about trying to sleep?*

Me: *We've talked about this. But give it a try if you want. I'm off.*

Me: *Where to?*

Me: *Anywhere but here. You're doing my head in, man.*

Yes, it's true; I'm doing my own head in. And there'll be fisticuffs at dawn unless I sort something pretty soon. Just not sure which horse to back if I don't.

29

THE RECYCLIST

I blame it all on Bradley. Cycling was so much cooler when it wasn't cool.

ILLUSTRATION:
MARTIN RIDGWELL

The Recyclist

Anyone out there that has built up a photofit of your humble author probably wouldn't have me down as a natural when it comes to all things cycling. And you'd be bang on the money, in truth; the booze-sodden carcass I carry around with me is probably best suited to more sedentary activities such as beekeeping or G4S security. So imagine my surprise when the exact same bicycle I'd had stolen in 2004 appeared in my eBay search field the other day. In Huddersfield, no less! And despite my advancing years and shocking loss of flexibility in the lumbar region, I decided it was to be mine. Which indeed it was – huzzah!

Now, if it hasn't already come to your attention, a lot has changed since 2004. Gone are the days when you could rock up at your local bike shop, stick your fag out in the plant pot outside and make a purchase without the slightest hint of embarrassment about jeans being tucked into socks. Not any more. Bike shops aren't even called bike shops. They are Performance Centres, where every nuance of your basic humanity is considered a weakness, to be overcome with specialist assistance from a Wiggly Braggins-a-like, employed to seek out your Achilles' heel and exploit it until the pips squeak. Sore knees? Incorrectly fitted cleats. Sore arse? Spend £120+ and we'll sort it. And don't get me started on bad gash.

Anyway, I turned up at one of these places a couple of days ago, looking like the Hovis boy with added alcohol. Call me naive, but I thought it would be a quick in/out affair from which I'd come away with some fancy kit that would get the ladies clucking at work. Not a chance. As I pushed my new steed through the door, wheezing with exhaustion from the 0.3 mile trek, a young lady whisked it away and thrust it into a vertical rack. As mild panic set in, I became aware of an even younger man, pedalling as if his life depended on it on some kind of vast treadmill, in front of which was a video screen displaying French byroads which he was virtually navigating. So distracted was I by all of this, I failed to notice the craggy Australian in bulging shorts looming ominously in front of me, there to help me get the most from my cycling experience. Clearly I was a curio to him (as he was to me) and for a brief while we stood there, locked into our very own Bateman moment.

I cracked first. Of course I did. Making a shoddy excuse, I shot out of the premises and onto *terra firma*. No sideburns, no kit, but at least with a semblance of dignity. For no matter how hard they try, I shall never yield to the tyranny of Lycra. Never. And if I look a bit pants on the road, so be it.

30

THE DEMON GROG

My mother advised me not to include this one. So here you go.

ILLUSTRATION:
RICHARD CRIGHTON

The Demon Grog

Of all the relationships I've ever had, possibly the most difficult is the one I still hold with the booze. It's pretty shit, to be frank, and I didn't choose it either. My namesake grandfather died of it before I was born, as did my own father indirectly, and it will probably see me off prematurely if the snout doesn't get me first. Its claws are pan-generational, way outside the boundaries of logic and reason, and conveniently, a quick re-read of the above somehow absolves me of any outright guilt, thereby allowing me to persevere with more of the same in order to write dispassionately about it. As if that makes it OK. The obvious opener, filed by those close enough to be concerned, is this:

'Do you drink alone?'

And the most honest answer I can give is:

'Yes, I do. I drink alone out of preference. Because then, finally, the ever-present critical voices (which extend into every cranny of my existence) shut up long enough for me to be able to do the things I genuinely care about. Until I go down the opposite slope and couldn't give a toss any more. Can I get you a top-up?'

It's not what they want to hear. And those I've upset along the path (there have been a few) will see it as a romanticised excuse, along the lines of Sebastian in *Brideshead Revisited*, very much the architect of his own downfall despite every gift life bestowed upon him. Someone kindly gave me a book last Christmas. Called *The Trip To Echo Spring* by Olivia Laing, it discusses the troubled link so many writers have with the Demon Grog. Not that I have ever considered myself a *bona fide* writer, and thereby lies the problem. The very term has such powerful connotations that the unsure are crippled at the starting blocks, woefully reliant on whatever it takes to be taken seriously; until the crutch becomes counterproductive, by which time it's usually too late. Between these, I walk a fine line. If that glorious moment ever comes about when something I have created becomes a thing, I'll probably be too mullered to notice. But maybe you will, and I'd be grateful if you could let me know. We've been around the block together for nearly four years. You owe me.

I have a rule. When I spew this tosh out, usually late at night and alongside a bottle of Pinot, I resist the temptation to hit the publish button until the following morning. Because, no matter how cathartic it may seem at the time, the unforgiving light of a new day will unfailingly reveal my incisive efforts to be little more than a muddled, steaming pile of cack. But ask yourselves something: you're reading this. Does that mean it's through quality control, or am I slumped comatose over the return key?

I'll leave that one with you.

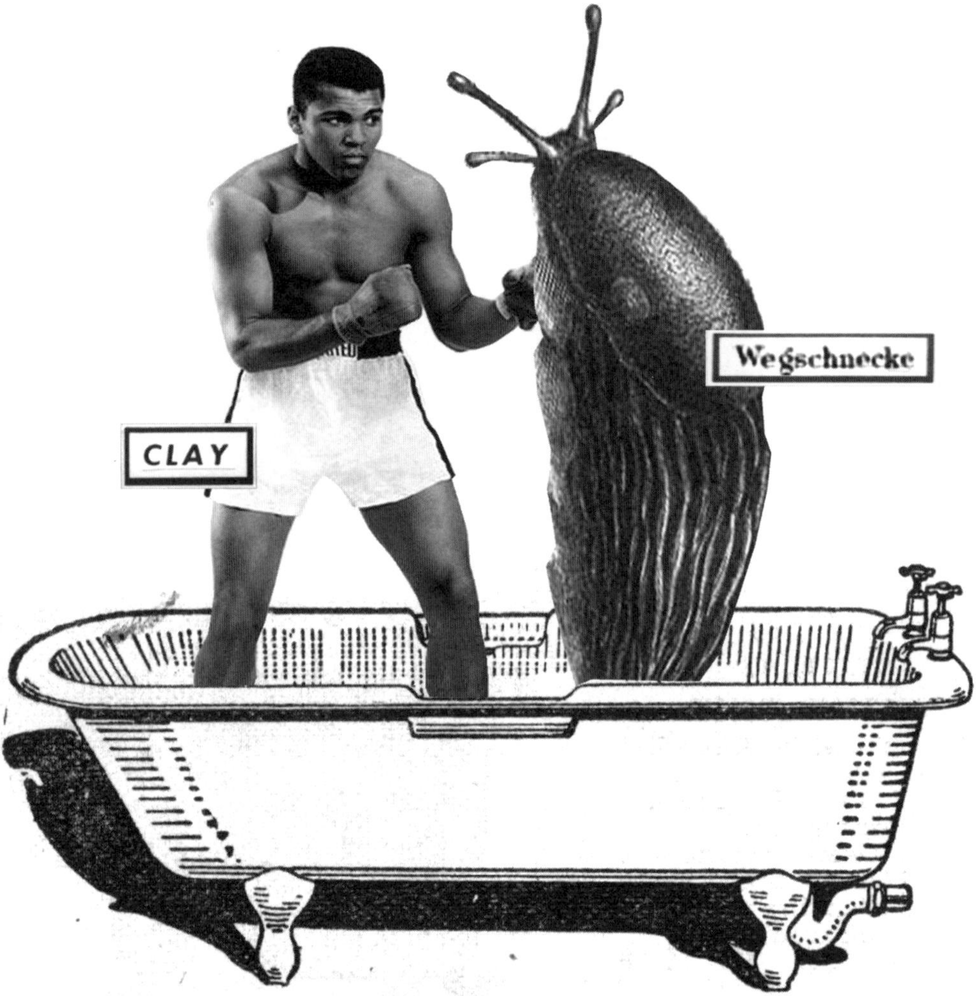

THE "FRANCIS" BATH WITH 12-in. SOAP-SINKINGS

31

THE SLUG IN HISTORY

Slugs, along with gerbils, spiders and foxes, always get a bad rap. This was my attempt at redressing the balance with the help of some spurious facts.

ILLUSTRATION:
PETER QUINNELL

The Slug in History

Q: *What did the slug say to the snail?*

A: *Big Issue, sir?*

I like slugs, me. Honestly. They don't do themselves any favours, but that's probably the reason we have cemented a conspiratorial bond of sorts over the years. They are the turds of the undergrowth, loathed by pretty much everyone for being brown and in the way. Even your most bog-standard, single-celled organism bristles when they meet on a glistening pavement, and would probably win if they got into fisticuffs. I know, I know, it's a tall order this one, but historically the slug has earned its spurs.

1911. The Pageant of London – in conjunction with the Festival of Empire – celebrated everything and anything that promoted the extraordinary advancement of the land. Highlight of which was the all-singing, all-dancing Tower of Slug, anchored in the Crystal Palace Gardens and seen by more than 15 million people over its lifetime. This magnificent structure was brown and got in the way for decades until it was destroyed in 1936. Because it was in the way.

In 1917, when resources were scarce and the Hun were menacingly close to Blighty, the good people of Folkestone erected a massive sea-front barricade constructed entirely of foraged molluscs, penetrable by neither sea nor air. Believing this blubbery mountain to be a cunning decoy, the Germans shifted their assault to the piers of Brighton, where they were annihilated conclusively at the slot machines.

It was considered 'good luck' for top racing drivers to keep a brace of slugs in their top pockets throughout the course of the Circuit de Monaco from 1909 until the controversy of 1966, when the first three finishers were disqualified for substitution with heavy slices of pork luncheon meat, illegal at the time.

Muhammad Ali (or Cassius Clay) enjoyed a bathtub filled to the brim with slugs local to the East Grinstead area throughout his most potent years. It is notable that before his classic bout with Joe Frazier in Manila 1975, he chose to replace British slugs with those hand-picked from his home town of Louisville, Kentucky USA.

In July 2007, when smoking was tentatively banned throughout the UK in all enclosed work spaces and a couple of years before the cynical advent of vaping, the fashionable young people of Hoxton, London tried their hands at 'sliming'. Popular at illegal raves and office parties, this required the slimer to balance the faux-fag at the fulcrum of two fingers whilst talking twaddle to anyone in the vicinity. Preferably with a beard.

And that's just scratching the surface. If you want the real dirt, go online: there's acres of info on the slug in history should you care to seek it out. I am merely the catalyst, the weaver if you will, my sole purpose being to prevent the denigration of our upstanding slimy pals. Until they get in the way.

32

THE RIGHT STUFF

I've gone badly off the whole 'cute brand' thing since this was written. These people are not my friends and I'm perfectly capable of buying wine on my own. Also quite happy with anything that stays down.

ILLUSTRATION:
KETTA MORRIS

The Right Stuff

Someone called William rang yesterday. Before he got through, I screened the number. Unfamiliar, but at least not one of those 08547 deals which you instantly know will come with a three second delay, over which you politely say '*Hello*' twice despite your better judgement, followed by an upbeat recorded message giving you just enough info on that accident you had to prevent you hanging up on the spot. Which you do regardless.

In short, William's prefix looked legit so I took the call, thinking it might be confirmation of my banking details from a new Nigerian business partner. His opening gambit was something along the lines of '*How are you?*' Now, as this particular question rarely arises, be it from my siblings, employer or accountant, I was half his already. Next came the introduction. Apparently, he is my personal wine advisor and was making a courtesy call based on the preferences made with my online account which, you may be surprised to learn, comes in at less than £200 per annum. He accurately noted that I enjoy wines from New Zealand, and proceeded to suggest a few others that may have escaped my notice. And despite all prior knowledge of the ruthlessness of marketing and cold-call grooming, I began to warm to him.

How we laughed at the crudity of your supermarket Shiraz. And how effortlessly he dropped in the buyer's sweet spot, being that place on the quality curve when you are no longer paying off taxes, duty and whatnot. The one when you go '*Hell, I'm worth £2.50*' and buy a couple of blue labels, as opposed to the plebeian red. And, in case I was still in any shadow of doubt, he reminded me that I would be fully refunded if his recommendations fell at all short. Geezer! I wanted to French kiss him down the phone, or at least ask him out for a pizza. This man knew more about me than my teachers from the 1980s or, dare I say it, my parents. And in my loved-up state, I saw us enjoying a mutual glass of an astonishingly rare Pinot under a wide Andalusian sunset.

But then came the crash. I nipped round to my friend Nick's house not long afterwards (who happens to be a marketing guru), so I told him about William and how it felt to be understood so completely. '*It's not what you think*', I protested. He gave me the skunk eye, then the lowdown on cute brands and upselling. You know, the sort of thing that companies like Innocent use to get you on team. And in an instant, the wonderful man-love I had experienced but hours before evaporated like acetone. I felt cheated, violated, abused. I thought he was different. I thought he was special. I thought he cared. So I ordered some more wine. The right stuff.

SHOP TIL U DRÖP

33

THE BRITISH AISLES

Booze aisles are scant reward for the hours of your life lost to feigning interest in food. But they'll do for now.

ILLUSTRATION:
DIGITAL PRIMATE

The British Aisles

I've just been to Sainsbury's. Not a dramatic admission, granted, but worthy of inclusion here because it got me to thinking about the partition that divides the connoisseur of fine beverages with significant alcohol content, and your more Hogarthian consumer. And let's be honest, it's pretty slim. Let me clear this one up a bit for the benefit of any readership that may have already embarked on their own aberrant journey.

Of all the aisles of one's supermarket of choice, the couple that supply the grape and the grain are surely the most well trodden. Here, there exists a curiously British microclimate, quite unlike any other. Grown men dramatically slow as they approach this particular section, their velocity utterly dependent on whether they are shopping alone or with a significant other. If it is the former, you can be fairly confident that a brewers Vintage Ale will slip itself into the basket and be justified at a later time. Approximately 8.5% volume and in a presentation box to boot.

From here, you leisurely browse the higher shelves, occasionally releasing the odd bottle for closer inspection. To the untrained eye this appears to be the hallmark of experience, but to the seasoned drinker all the signs are there. A deft handspin clearly suggests that the vintner has erroneously slapped alcohol volume to the rear, whilst the inclusion of two or more bottles of the same product tends to signify some kind of sordid bin end deal, from which neither distributor nor end user comes up smelling of roses.

Next up is hard liquor, always a tough one. These shimmering beauties in their idiosyncratic shapes and sizes, all vying for your attention, require more than a modicum of discipline if you are to make it through the rest of the day unscathed. Probably best to give them a miss, but

Santa Maria! They so have your balls in a vice! Maybe this small Italian one, distilled by monks in mountain ranges many miles from civilisation? Or this square baby from Tennessee, originally conceived by a philanthropic hillbilly with a beard as long as your arm? Go on, you know you want to, and what's the worst that can happen? Then there's the agony of the mixer. The one that's been around since the '70s usually does the trick, but right next to it there's another that says it's organic, natural and poured over the thighs of virgins for added flavour. Probably. Screw it, it's going in x12.

It's at this point you become aware that you are not alone. A young man with facial growth that needs attention has clocked your basket and is shooting you a look: empathy. His own contains a few tins of own-brand cider, total value of which is one thirtieth of yours. But here, in this sacred space, all discrepancies bleed into themselves and alcohol, just this once, becomes the great leveller.

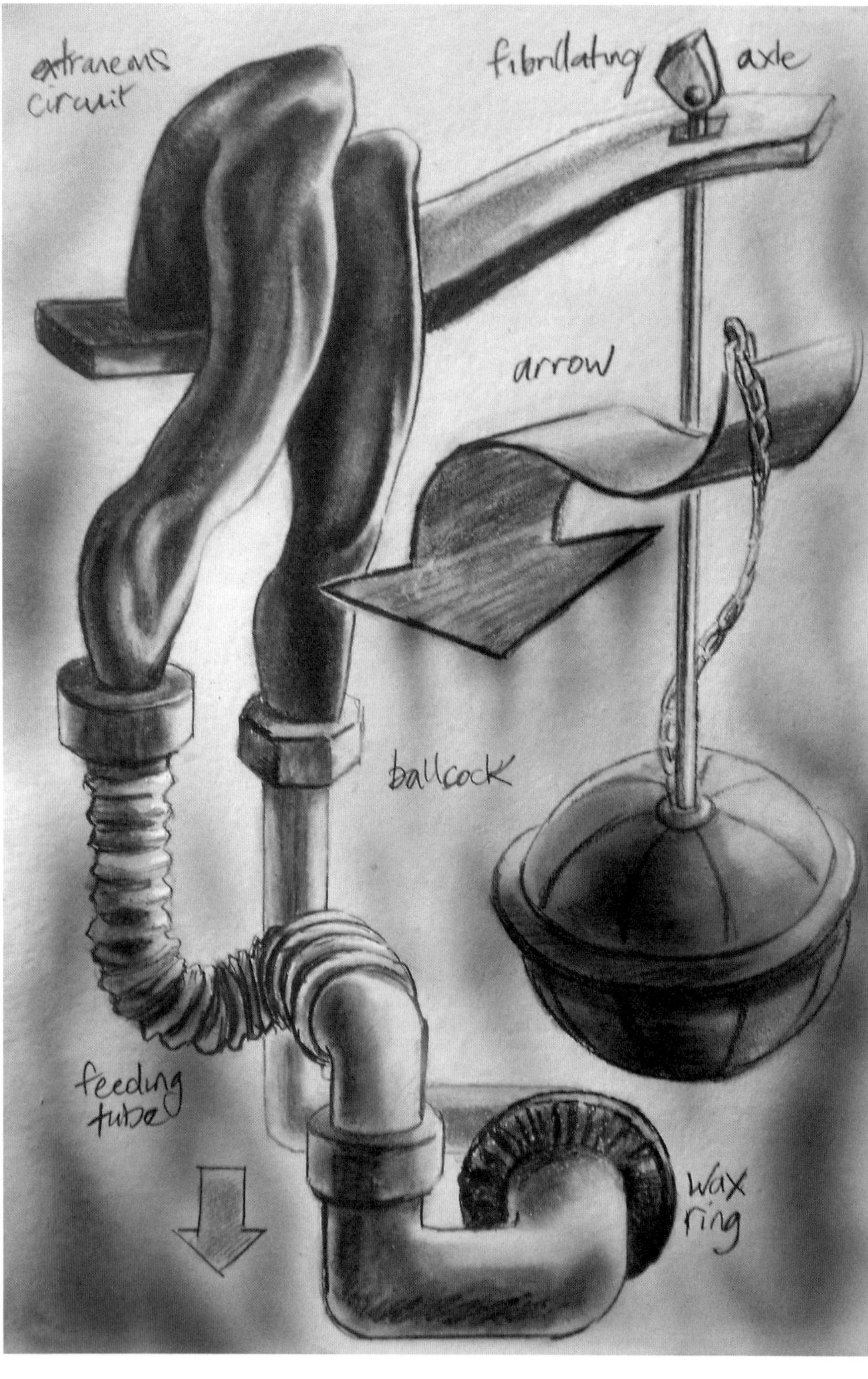
extraneous circuit
fibrillating axle
arrow
ballcock
feeding tube
wax ring

34

THE BLOO LOO

The myth that DIY desperados can tackle home plumbing issues is successfully debunked here. Tradesmen aren't expensive for nothing.

ILLUSTRATION:
REBECCA PARKIN

The Bloo Loo

Some of you may be familiar with the ignominy of dealing with the occasional nocturnal plumbing malfunction, by which I am not referring to the incessant failings of the male anatomy in its twilight years. No, last night offered me the luxury of delving deep into the cistern of my lavatory to block off the overflow, thereby preventing a subsequent tsunami of waste too disturbing to contemplate in the small hours (or at any other time for that matter). Despite having the incorrect tools to hand, I managed to wedge a family-sized Toilet Duck bottle in there somehow and fiddled about with an entry-level spanner until I got bored and went to bed. *No need for a tradesman's call-out, I'm all over this one. Thank you very much.*

However, this morning presented me with a couple of extra problems not oft encountered by the more experienced plumber. For starters, my arms were indelibly stained with the remnants of a Bloo Max Loo tablet, purchased on the promise that it would provide a cascade of fresh blue water for up to two months, but failing to alert the customer as to its potential Smartwater association should the have-a-go hero get involved at the business end. Vigorous scrubbing at the sink only made matters worse, as semi-dissolved globs of gunk flew up into my face and onto my person, leaving me resembling a bargain basement, wannabe Smurf. Oh, and I managed to smash the lav lid into three violent-looking shards due to incorrect posture in the ire of despair.

At this point, your less plucky DIYer would probably have thrown in the towel. Understandably so. But I was undeterred. A quick spruce up in the shower and a brisk march over to Plumbase was all I needed to get my spunk back. The opaque black bag I took with me contained an unappealing red valve spare which could well have been half-inched from Ann Summers, but I was confident it held all the clues I needed to secure a healthy tank by midday. Wrong.

Me: *Good morning! I wonder if you could help me? Do you have a washer for this cistern plunger?*

Plumbase: *What's a cistern plunger, then?*

Me: *Er… it's this. It just goes into the… er… down part. You know, inside the top. And it's leaking. I'm sure it's perfectly simple.*

Plumbase: *Is it one of ours?*

Me: *I'm sorry?*

Plumbase: *One of ours. Y'know, Royal Doulton, Twyford, Ideal and the like.*

Me: *You mean British?*

Plumbase: *Don't stock the competition.*

Me: *I see. I don't think it has a label.*

Plumbase: *Can't help you then, mate. By the way, you've got blue all ov…*

Me: *Yes, I know.*

Smarting from the latent xenophobia of the high street, I returned home to do battle in the small room. For I would say to my house, as I said to those who served in Plumbase: '*I have nothing to offer but blood, toil, tears and sweat*'. And Bloo Max.

ADVERTISEMENT
The Sting.
by Vango
"NO POLES REQUIRED"

35

THE STiNG

Shades of Stella Street. I liked the idea that the rickety table by the loos in my brother's pub was a Live Aid favourite. It is also worth mentioning that most evenings spent there invariably end with his murdering of Wonderwall on the acoustic.

ILLUSTRATION:
TIM SIDDALL

The Sting

Mrs Sting: *Is that the Idle Hour?*

Me: *It certainly is. How can I help?*

Mrs Sting: *It's Mrs Sting here. You know, the other half.*

Me: *Hello Mrs Sting. Would you like to book a table?*

Mrs Sting: *No, not exactly. But I could use your help. It's a somewhat delicate matter.*

Me: *It's not the, er, tantric business again, is it?*

Mrs Sting: *I'm afraid it is. And he's getting worse. I haven't slept in over a week and I was rather hoping you could recommend something to dampen his ardour, so to speak.*

Me: *Of course. Well, the organic chicken thighs washed down with one of our biodynamic reds should do the trick. Mr and Mrs Meatloaf were in over bank holiday and they had to be airlifted home afterwards.*

Mrs Sting: *I don't think so. Any mention of thighs and he'll be at it like a rat up a drainpipe. No, I was thinking of something a little more sedative.*

Me: *How about our Stroh 80% volume Austrian rum? Pop a couple of shots in his coffee when he's out pointing Percy and he won't be bothering you for quite some time.*

Mrs Sting: *Been there. He bought a case back after the last European tour and whipped through it like lemonade. Gave a whole new meaning to Viennese Whirl though.*

Me: *Hmm, difficult one. How's the book going, by the way?*

Mrs Sting: *That's precisely the problem! I don't have five seconds to myself anymore. The minute I sit down at the computer he gets all hot under the collar and chases me round the mansion like in 'The Secretary'. I'm only on the preface and I'm exhausted already.*

Me: *Can I make another suggestion?*

Mrs Sting: *Please do. I'm at my wits' end.*

Me: *It's a long shot but it might have legs. I've been working here for a while now and when we get stragglers at the end of a shift, Nibs hops onto the acoustic and anaesthetises them with his astonishing rendition of 'Wonderwall'. Works every time!*

Mrs Sting: *Perfect! I'll get the chopper out.*

Me: *Isn't that what we're trying to avoid, Mrs Sting?*

Mrs Sting: *No, I mean I'll bring him over tonight. Book me a table for two by the traps.*

Me: *Slight problem. Mr and Mrs Bono have already reserved the traps table. Popular one with the Live Aid lot, it seems.*

Mrs Sting: *Listen, I want that table. Do what you have to, OK? If it helps, I'll do a book reading in your bloody pub when I've done it. Got that? Good. And clear a space in the garden for the chopper. I mean, the helicopter.*

Mrs Sting will be reading excerpts from her frank autobiography *One Swallow Does Not A Sumner Make* in the Idle Hour Rest Rooms when she has written it. All rights reserved © Ward 10 Books, including the made-up bits. Especially them.

DOWNTON ABBEY
UNCON

36

THE ENGLISH STRAITJACKET

Hugh, what have you done to us?

ILLUSTRATION:
SASCHA GRAVENSTEIN

The English Straitjacket

Sometimes being English is plain awful. The absolute pits. Yes, yes, I know we're all terribly polite and good at pop music, being ironic and making the most of our crappy weather, but when it comes to saying what we actually mean, we are lamentably backward. How often have you apologised for someone else's rudeness? For being in the way when you never were? Or pretended things are just fine when your internal tolerance needle has just over tipped into the red?

I do it frequently. At the end of pretty much every cold call received (over which I weakly feign surprise at that accident I never had, or the very specific amount the banks owe me for insurance I never took out), I hear myself thanking a computerised voice for its time and, on occasion, wishing it a pleasant day. Which only serves to fill mine with self-loathing and misanthropy. And, cliché though it may be, I constantly find myself drawn to queues, quite often for something I have no interest in at all. Why? *Why?*

Because it reaffirms the quintessence of our Englishness, and that Englishness broods deep inside us all, gnawing away at baser attributes such as anger and self-confidence, until all that is left is the quivering bag of neuroses we move around inside every day. It is a curious evolutionary quirk, for if shifted over to the animal kingdom, your average Brit would be mercilessly and fatally mauled before he/she had finished blinking. Probably by something French or Polish, whose very means of survival hinges on the exact opposite.

Speaking of France, here's another example. When I was fifteen, I was placed at a school in Toulouse for a short while. There, I came across a delightful young lady called Catherine Voisinet, who blushed when I was around and clearly wanted me to make the first move.

My French was adequate enough to facilitate this, and I was not yet marred by a forthcoming volcano of acne. But did I? Of course I didn't. I just sat around, blushing back at her in English until she got bored and started dating a Neanderthal rugby player with grazed knuckles. Who thought I was '*un con*'. And he was probably right.

I'd love to be able to tell you that it'll all turn out OK. That *being a bit Hugh Grant* isn't such a bad thing, and that more bullish nations will sneakingly admire you for all that pent-up emotion. But I fear that would be a lie. It is, and they don't, despite what you may have been led to believe from the inexplicable overseas success of *Downton Abbey* and the like. They're collecting ammo for the next way to shaft us rotten, based on information we willingly throw at them. Then they'll steal our ideas, market our booze, buy up our housing stock etc… and repackage it all as their own. And we'll probably thank them for it.

A laminated tray with a cat on it.

37

THE JOY OF B&B

As a conservator, I've stayed in more of these than I care to discuss. Perhaps their Air equivalent will see them off but I doubt it. What would we have left to moan about if they totally vanished?

ILLUSTRATION:
SARAH EVANS

The Joy of B&B

One of the perennial delights available to the migrant worker in the UK is that of the great British B&B. In an age of flux, it is comforting to note that this cultural constant has roots deep enough to weather the whims of fancy and will remain defiantly crap until the end of time. And if anyone is in any doubt about this, check out *Rising Damp* on Comedy Gold before giving it a go. OK, let's start at the top.

A significant percentage of any annual B&B budget goes on *external appearance*, making it the Joan Collins of temporary accommodation. This leaves very little once you're inside but by this point the transaction has generally been made online, leaving the hapless punter at the mercy of the Fury within (which I shall come to presently).

The room. Generally converted from an underused alcove into a Laura Ashley-inspired floral extravaganza, complete with Morphy Richards kettle on a laminated tray with a cat on it, sugar sachets nicked from the nearest Wetherspoons and some UHT milk. The light switch will *NEVER* be where it should and only two of the floorboards covered by the Rorschach purple carpet will not creak, making a mockery of you and your endless trips to the bathroom (which I shall come to presently).

Sod it, I'll come to it now. *The bathroom* is, by default, at the furthest point in the building from where you happen to be. Don't ever question this, it's just how it is. And no amount of corridor-creeping will prevent other guests being aware and in full audio range of your intended business, be it a shower, a widdle or a go on the throne. If it is the latter, may I recommend leaving a tap running? This affords the end user the camouflage of a decaying Edwardian plumbing system, screaming to keep up with modern-day demands as you wrestle to silence your most basic of emissions.

Breakfast. If you, like me, have learned to get by on a monstrously strong cup of Colombian and a couple of fags, you're going to be in for a shock. Your host will be frying up a wealth of sizzling flesh, surrounded by dogs and photographs of horses from the 1970s. Dietary deviations from the above will be frowned upon, as will quantity. Even going all frightfully awfully doesn't cut much mustard here, so you'll just have to suffer the consequences.

The internet. This extraordinary modern miracle is not much understood at your B&B which is why they tend to turn it off at night. Like in the war. However, they know you'll go elsewhere if it's not there so you do have the upper hand.

Finally, just remember: if you crack and report these *ailing establishments* to whatever ombudsman you adhere to, they'll go the same way as slavery, capital punishment and underage drinking. On your own heads be it.

Tim
DAAS

38

THE OMEN

Relentless anxiety dreams of impending death and being a bit crap in the sack. Although better than being awake with same, it must be said.

ILLUSTRATION:
TIM FERGUSON

The Omen

I've been having insane dreams of late. Seriously out there. One of them had a friend of mine serving sandwiches in a cricket pavilion as it filled up to the ceiling with water, and another saw me crossing an Egyptian desert, half-starved, bug-eyed and decomposing under the searing heat. I may be mistaken, but I'm pretty sure the subconscious is kicking off big time and I have no idea what it's trying to tell me. The fact that I've been off the tuck for a while could be a contributing factor, but let's be honest, that's why we have cigarettes. No, it is surely something more sinister, possibly to do with the Grim Reaper, and I've done next to nothing to prevent my untimely demise. And when I say next to nothing, I mean nothing.

The trouble with getting stuck in this mindset is that once you're there, just about everything becomes an augury of one's own final exit. My recent trip to the doctor is the most obvious, but less pertinent events can still give me the willies. A black cat looking at me funny doesn't mean I'm going to cop it, or at least it shouldn't. And when two crows run off like the clappers across the park, it's highly likely they've seen a worm or a mouse in the borders and are not the harbingers of doom I've concocted in my head. Even the washing up can get ominous, particularly when a knife clatters to the floor, spins around a few times and gurgles '*Redrum! Redrum!*' from the back of its non-existent larynx. It's a miracle I get up in the mornings.

I mentioned the above to said friend (who happens to be interested in the significance of dreams), and she put me at ease a little. Fortunately, that room filling up with water does not represent imminent death. Not at all. Rather, it suggests deeply suppressed sexual anxiety and an unsuccessful battle with evil, foreshadowing trouble, sickness and misery. Phew! And as for the other one, well that says something or other about my dissatisfaction with present companions and employment. Yeah, whatever. At least I'll still be around to hate them when I get sacked.

Just before my great-grandmother passed away, I remember visiting her bedside in a small suburban house in Surrey. She was on the verge, but still pretty lucid. And we were having a chinwag, like you do when you're six and talking to an old lady who smells of cabbages, when she suddenly sat bolt upright and pointed at a speck on the opposite wall. Her eyes were blazing, her hand trembling. I never found out what it was that irked her (she died shortly afterwards), but as I march towards the same place at breakneck speed, I do wonder if these visions become more real than life itself at the end. Or whether you just need a good wank and a sarnie.

PIERRE'S PINKY
MANO MELINDA
PHILIPPA
TRISH
SIMON
LE FIN
MARK

39

THE CONTRACTUAL OBLIGATION

Exactly what it says. The respective Kickstarter pledgers will be rueing the day they parted with their hard-earned cash. Ever get the feeling you've been had?

ILLUSTRATION:
MARK WEIGHTON

The Contractual Obligation

Right, the book fundraising is officially done and dusted. Time to roll up my sleeves and make the bloody thing, and if you're reading this from a weighty tome and not online, you'll know that somehow I pulled it off. But lovely though it may be to have the printing dosh in the bag, I do have other contractual issues to consider. For example, I promised Philippa Burne, Trish Dicey and Simon Phipps that I'd write them all into a book post and now that we're out of the blocks, I haven't a clue how to do it. I mean, they've never met each other and they all live in different countries for starters. So it's not as if I could set up a chance encounter in a supermarket or nightclub, is it? No, I'm going to have to be way smarter than that. And possibly a tad duplicitous.

I've also told Melinda Doring and Pierre Woollard that they will be illustrated by the godlike hand of Mark Weighton, and I got to thinking I could somehow shoehorn the whole lot of them in together. No one will be any the wiser and my workload would effectively be halved. Confused? I know, I know. But what if Mark does this drawing of me scribbling away at my desk and there, legibly on the paper, are three names: Philippa, Trish and Simon. I'm lost in the muse, brow furrowed and clearly on edge. As per. Fortunately, Melinda is there pouring me a glass of Pinot and Pierre is carrying a ramekin of liquorice in from the kitchen. See, it's brilliant! All bases are covered and I get a night off.

Obviously, this cunning ploy is fully dependent on Mark stepping up to the plate. Because if he locks horns and does something different, my cover will be blown and I'll have to do it again, which kind of defeats the object. So I'll tell him the pledge specifically states that he does all the graft and bank on him being too busy to check. He's an artist, as if he would. Next, I contact everyone concerned and tell them the good news. What's not to like? I surpass myself sometimes, I really do.

In case you're wondering, it isn't easy being this Machiavellian. A lot of time and effort goes in at the deep end. Thinking about it, probably about the same amount of time and effort to just do it properly and skip out the cod cloak-and-dagger nonsense entirely. But that's not the point, is it? I have an obligation to my pledgers and I shall fulfil it by whatever convoluted method is necessary. And if it so happens to make my life considerably easier, well that's the way the cookie crumbles.

My brighter readers will have spotted what I did there. But that's between us and it goes no further. A lot hangs on this, capiche?

40

THE LONELINESS OF THE LONG DISTANCE PIZZA FLYER DELIVERY BOY

A little Christmas cheer to end with. I see these guys from my study occasionally (they're usually guys), and often wonder what it must feel like to be pedalling a product no one wants.

ILLUSTRATION:
MARK DICEY

The Loneliness of the Long Distance Pizza Flyer Delivery Boy

The bundle arrives at 5am. Dan and Charlie don't come in, they never do, just sling it down by the milk crates and drive off. It's usually wet when I pick it up but it don't matter, I throw the top and bottom ones out anyway. Saves about twenty minutes in the long run. Not recently, though. They've put the big houses up on the Ridge onto my round 'cos it's the holidays and no one's about. Takes bloody ages to get up there and they've all got them 'No Junk Mail' signs so you know you're not wanted. Sometimes one of 'em comes out and shouts but you just pretend you don't hear nothing and keep going. No time to stop, too cold for that. Just get it over with.

Nan's got me some gloves for Christmas. The thermal ones, she said, to stop me pinkies going blue. Trouble is, you can't sort through the flyers so you only end up taking them off, bless her. Sometimes I go round after I'm done 'cos she's always got the heating up. Like the Bahamas in there most days, even in summer. Might nip over later if it's still light. She likes a natter.

The first bit's dead quick. Mostly flats, all shoved up close together and no one cares if you chuck in some extras. They all end up in the bin, so what's a few more if it makes life easier? You've got to watch it, though. A couple of lads got the elbow for putting theirs in a skip last week and bunking off early; not what you want at this time of year. Usually you see a few posties on the way, struggling with their big sacks of parcels and fat letters and cards and that. Makes you glad you're not one of them, even though they make loads more than us. We don't talk, neither. Everyone wants to get back indoors, quick as you like.

As you move out of town, the houses get bigger and further apart. Some have drives you've got to walk up, and dogs giving it all that until you leave. And those letterboxes that snap back onto your fingers, 'cos to them you're no better than the draughts they're keeping out. There's usually someone in, but when they see you coming they go in another room and pretend they're not there. You can see their shadows through the crazy glass, trying to keep still. When you finally get up to the Ridge, you know you're on the home run. Grand old places all the way along it, but there's not too many and it's downhill all the way back. You're glad of this 'cos by now you've had enough.

Today though, this old geezer comes out of one in his pyjamas and it's well after lunch. 'Here we go', I says, and pull up my hood. But he's shouting and shouting and I'm thinking maybe I've dropped something outside, so I go back. He's only holding a tray and offering it out to me like some bloody weirdo. Now, I've been told about this sort of thing back at the depot and how to deal with it, but he don't look so bad. Quite sad, actually. 'Happy Christmas', he goes. 'Have a mince pie. It'll keep you warm'. I'm looking at him harsh so he don't think I'm one of them, but he's right: it's bloody freezing and it'll be an hour or two before I get back. So I take the pie and it's lovely and warm in my hands. I watch him take a bite of his so I know it's alright, then I put the whole thing in my mouth and swallow it down quick. And it's proper nice. All sugary sweet with raisins and fruit and everything. But then I look up to say cheers and the bastard's gone back in. Like I said, bloody weirdo.

Don't think I'll make it over to Nan's after all. It's getting dark and I'm up early in the morning. She'll wait a day and you know what? That pie will do me until I get in, and the streetlights sort of make you feel warm too. It's not so bad. And it's downhill all the way back.

***

ILLUSTRATION:
TIM SIDDALL

THE ARTiSTS

01 The DnA Factory | Artists

The DnA Factory is the collaborative practice of Dallas & Angel, established in the early '90s after graduating from Goldsmiths College. Working in the fields of sculptural assemblage, installation, collage and photomontage, their work is a hybrid of Surreal- Pop and Baroque, merging observational reality with myth and story telling. The DnA Factory are Members of the Royal British Society of Sculptors.

www.thednafactory.com

02 Ursula McLaughlin | Graphic Designer

Long-suffering designer who says 'yes' to projects without thinking it through first. She is hoping to get her reward in heaven.

ursula.mcl@gmail.com

03 Anthony Reynolds | Musician/Author

Anthony Reynolds writes books, music, songs and shopping lists which he then tears up, burns and flushes down the toilet.

www.anthonyreynolds.net

04 Claire Fletcher | Illustrator

Claire studied at the Royal College of Art and illustrates anything from children's books and Easter egg boxes, to articles about current affairs. She is co-founder and director of *Made in Hastings*, a shop selling her own and other people's stuff and she sells paintings from her shed, *The Black Winkle*, in Hastings Old Town.

www.clairefletcherart.com

05 Magda Archer | Artist/Printmaker

Magda Archer is an artist and printmaker who studied at Ravensbourne College of Art, Chelsea School of Art and the Royal College of Art. She has yet to produce the necessary certificates to authenticate these claims.

www.magdaarcher.com

06 Nick Hollywood | Musician/Producer

Nick is a musician, designer, DJ, radio presenter and head honcho at Freshly Squeezed Music. Described as a 'suave impresario' by *The Independent* and 'the Godfather of Electro Swing' by *The Daily Telegraph*, he has recently launched a new joint venture label (Vintage Remix) in partnership with Island Records.

www.freshlysqueezedmusic.com

07 Dan Laidler | Musician/Artist/Sage

Dan spends much of his time out walking in the countryside around his home, contemplating some of the more mysterious aspects of human nature. He has very little patience for arty-farty bullshit.

www.danlaidler.com

08 Matt Jeffs | Designer/Illustrator

Matt (who goes by Nimbws as googling 'Matt Jeffs' would bring up Matt and Jeff's Car Wash in Southern California) works as a freelance designer and illustrator. Carving out a niche working with the beer industry, a lot of his meetings tend to happen in pubs. His work styles take a lot from Cubism, German Expressionism and Comic Books.

www.nimbws.co.uk

09 Martin Ridgwell | Artist/Printmaker

Martin trained in printmaking at several studios and studied for his Masters at the University of the Arts London. He was awarded the Gwen May Student Prize from the Royal Society of Painter Printmakers (RE) in 2006 and made a Full Fellow in 2008. He was an original member of the London Printmakers, exhibits regularly at major galleries and his work is held in national and international collections. He lives and works in London.

www.martinridgwell.co.uk

10 Richard Crighton | Designer/Illustrator/Musician

Richard is a creative car crash of a man, swerving from catastrophe to catastrophe with all the confidence of a sleepwalking orangutan. This clearly marks a new low.

www.crighton.de

11 Peter Quinnell | Illustrator

Peter Quinnell has been doing collage and assemblage for illustration and art since the 1980s, and has worked with a galaxy of star clients.

peterquinnell@gmail.com

www.debutart.com

12 Ketta Morris | Graphic Designer

Ketta works in some sort of design job. But most of her time is spent dancing, shopping and occasionally drawing birthday cards because she's too tight to buy them. She doesn't have a website but does have a Twitter account and would like more followers.

@kettamorris

13 Digital Primate | Musician

Digital Primate is a techno dilettante currently residing in Amsterdam where he runs an electronic music production studio for other techno dilettantes. In recent years he has been commissioned to provide artwork for electronic record label Desolat, and has shown his work in Subway Gallery in London. He makes techno music, mainly.

www.digitalprimate.com

14 Rebecca Parkin | Artist

Rebecca Parkin makes paintings, collages and drawings, influenced by science fiction, fantasy art, comic books and video games. These genres provide her with an ideal terrain with which to explore the borders between fantasy and gender construction. She studied her MA at the Royal College of Art and currently has a studio in north London.

www.rebeccaparkin.co.uk

15 Tim Siddall | Artist/Musician/Poet

AKA Flame Proof Moth, AKA Poet For Hire, AKA That Bloke Who Sings In The Thames.

Eccentric performer available for high-profile support slots now.

www.timsiddall.com

www.flameproofmoth.com

www.poetforhire.net

16 Sascha Gravenstein | Artist/Graphic Designer

Sascha lives and works in London.

www.saschagravenstein.com

17 Sarah Evans | Designer/Illustrator

Sarah lives, works and makes pictures in Mid-Wales.

sarahevansdesign@hotmail.com

18 Tim Ferguson | Comedian/Author

The Doug Anthony All-Stars are an Australian art collective first established in 1927. Tim wrote bestseller manual '*The Cheeky Monkey – Writing Narrative Comedy*' [Currency Press]. He works with DAAS comedy.

www.cheekymonkeycomedy.com

19 Mark Weighton | Artist

For over two decades, Mark Weighton has been creating artworks which explore a vision of the interconnected nature of existence. From his studio in West Sussex, he has exhibited work both nationally and internationally, and features in many private art collections across Europe and the Americas.

www.markweighton.com

20 Mark Dicey | Artist

Mark is a Canadian artist who makes paintings and drawings. He also collaborates with other artists, such as the drawing trio *Drunken Paw* and the collaborative group *Aeolian Recreational Boundary Institute*.

www.markdicey.ca

* * *